The FIRE *and the* SILENCE

The FIRE *and the* SILENCE

PRAYER, THOUGHT, *and the* BATTLE *for* INNER STILLNESS

Fr. John Henry Hanson, O. Praem.

Foreword by Tammy M. Peterson

Published by Scepter Publishers, Inc.

info@scepterpublishers.org
www.scepterpublishers.org
800-322-8773
New York

Cover Design: DeLight Design Studio
Text Design and Pagination: PerfecType

Paperback ISBN: 978-1-59417-108-6
Ebook ISBN: 978-1-59417-114-7

Library of Congress Control Number: 2025947518

Printed in the United States of America

I went out to the hazel wood,
Because a fire was in my head . . .

—from “The Song of Wandering Aengus”
William Butler Yeats

CONTENTS

FOREWORD
Defined by Fire from Within

Recently, my four-year-old grandson had his first experience playing team sports. It was soccer, played in a park near our home. His focus was intense as he kept up with his team—until, that is, a garbage truck came around to empty the park's refuse containers. He stopped playing, mesmerized by the garbage truck. He did not look back to the game until the garbage truck moved past the field and out of sight.

The power of something as ordinary as a garbage truck to fascinate, even to divert attention away from a game, almost as though the game had ceased to exist, is amazing. It is also worth thinking about. What has the power to get and hold our attention?

From the pedestrian to the sublime . . . Jordan reflects on this phenomenon in connection with Moses and the burning bush, the most iconic moment of divine attention-grabbing:

> We are always seized by awe when we find ourselves in the grip of something; when our attention is focused, whether voluntarily or involuntarily, or in the strange situation where both are the case simultaneously: when

> we cannot help but notice, but then decide, of our own accord, to investigate.
>
> We are always compelled by variants of the burning bush; by the encounter with something that is both enduring in its being and furiously becoming, simultaneously. There is nowhere this happens more evidently than in the case of life itself, defined by its fire from within.*

Who can say why my grandson went from being engrossed in his game to being fascinated with refuse collection. But as the focal point of his interest, the garbage truck briefly functioned as a tool or instrument that might, someday, answer his call to action in the world. Like most little boys, my grandson saw the machinery and tools used by adult men as the tools of both maturity and manhood. Or maybe even more so, he saw them as the means by which men interact with the world as men.

His sister, only three years old, has naturally had a very different focus, a different fascination: a baby doll. When her mom was expecting her next baby, the little girl held the doll constantly, transporting it in a carriage or nursing it and changing its diaper. These are the tools of a mother, learned at the beginning of life, and my granddaughter is not so easily distracted from the "care" she delicately lavishes on her toy baby.

Tools or instruments are means to an end. They help us not only to express ourselves but also, more practically, to fix broken things or facilitate the use of any goal-directed activity or thing. The Victorian thinker and essayist Thomas Carlyle once

---

* Jordan B. Peterson, *We Who Wrestle with God: Perceptions of the Divine* (Portfolio/Penguin, 2024), pp. 95, 96.

offered a reductive definition of man as "a tool-using animal," and said that "without tools he is nothing, with tools he is all."* Like all reductive definitions, a partial truth emerges: Unlike other mammals, we use our intelligence in highly sophisticated ways to subdue the earth, advance technology, create artworks, and many other things. Not only do we use tools, but we make and refine them as need occasions.

The highest activity humans can perform is prayer. Its methods may be construed as "tools" of a sort. However, in the end, prayer is *relational* because its essence is love, loving communion and communication between God and the soul.

What I have said thus far about my grandchildren and their absorption by things meaningful to them reflects how prayer works, especially since a childlike spirit is a gospel prerequisite for entering the kingdom of God. Children get absorbed in their play to the point of obliviousness to everything else around them. Focus is almost effortless because they love what they're doing and are completely unselfconscious about it.

As we grow older, most of us find such focus an increasing struggle. Thoughts abound, and not always of the most helpful kinds. Prayer brings our inner discord into high relief: As we try to still the mind and heart, we find them darting off into worries, fears, desires, and the like. But is the problem really one of concentration, of focus? Will greater self-discipline secure greater attentiveness?

Over the course of my life I have developed tools that I call on to keep me grounded, in ways physical, emotional, and

---

* Thomas Carlyle, *Sartor Resartus* (1834), bk. 1, ch. 5.

spiritual. However, until I was introduced to Christian prayer, and especially the prayer of the Rosary, there was always something missing.

Just as my grandchildren enjoy playing their games, as a child I always loved outdoor games with my friends, playing from morning until night, coming in only after the streetlights came on. Baseball, swimming, and biking around town were some of my favorites. Jordan and I met in the third grade, and we soon joined forces in game-playing. Apart from outdoor games, he taught me to play chess. We were inseparable on the playground until I was twelve.

When I was twelve years old, our family home became kind of empty. My siblings left to go to university and my parents were busy working, curling or golfing in the evenings and on weekends. Around this age I stopped attending the Protestant church where I had gone each Sunday for services and Sunday school.

In the wake of this spiritual vacuum, I began the daily practice of meditation, but not in the Christian sense. My godmother had introduced me to yoga, and I learned to practice meditation in conjunction with its various postures. At the time, spiritual practices of the Far East were circulating in the culture. The Beatles had popularized aspects of Hindu spirituality in their music, with George Harrison introducing the Indian guitar-like sitar into some of their songs, such as "The Inner Light" and "Norwegian Wood." For four decades I practiced yoga exercises and meditation daily. The practice kept me physically fit and mentally grounded, and I thought the benefits of yoga would continue to be helpful as I aged.

After my teen years, I attended the University of Ottawa, where I graduated with a BSc in Kinesiology—a degree focused on anatomy and physiology that equipped me to work in massage therapy. In my spare time, I went to community art classes to practice life-drawing enriched by my growing knowledge of anatomy. A common theme of my interests, recognizable in retrospect, is a contemplative view of the human person and nature. Whether yoga had so disposed me for this or whether it is a personality feature, I can't say. But art certainly accustoms us to look deeply into the world around us.

It was also after I finished university that I went to Montreal to marry Jordan. We were inseparable once again, and this time for keeps. I remember traveling with him to a behavioral medicine conference, which I attended only as an observer. It was there that I met an anesthesiologist, Dr. Dharma Singh Khalsa, who practiced Kundalini yoga. Each morning he facilitated a 5:00 a.m. class called "Wake Up to Wellness." I thought it was a miracle that there was something at the conference for me.

The class was a sitting breathing meditation developed to bring up the "serpentine Kundalini energy" for the day. It purported to bring about spiritual energy and wisdom from the depths of one's being. I began to practice this routine every morning and also incorporated a Sun Salutation for physical wellness. It helped me stay calm in stressful situations and patient when, as a new mother, I was frequently short on sleep. All these tools worked together to support me throughout my nearly sixty years of life.

My experience of meditation and the interior life developed from these practices, normally cautioned against by Christian teaching but which nevertheless helped me acquire an initial taste for the interior life.* Flannery O'Connor once noted that many people come to the Church by means the Church does not allow. But on the other hand, if it were not for unallowable paths, the conversion process itself would be vitiated altogether. All of us are in need of continual conversion, a turning toward the Lord. The need to turn back, more or less, suggests one is (also more or less) off track.

Yoga introduced me to meditation as a way of clearing my mind of unwanted thoughts. I had been tormented by a need to control, a need to help others as a way to receive validation, and I had frequent thoughts of self-pity. Although yoga helped me in these ways, it did not allay my deeper "existential" confusion as to how to live the best life I could. I felt I was born for something greater and had some intuitions about prayer, yet it would be years before those intuitions would find their true expression, and especially find their nourishment in the readings and study of Sacred Scripture.

Everything changed when, at the age of fifty-seven, I was diagnosed with terminal kidney cancer and given only months to live. My former tools were insufficient to support me through this crisis.

---

* See Congregation for the Doctrine of the Faith, Letter to the Bishops of the Catholic Church on Some Aspects of Christian Meditation (October 15, 1989) which addresses doctrinal ambiguities while acknowledging the therapeutic use of certain eastern forms of meditation. https://www.vatican.va/.

I underwent surgery to remove half of my left kidney in March 2019. Although I recovered, I began to have flank pain. A biopsy of the remaining half of my kidney clarified the picture. When Jordan and I went to the surgeon for the six-week follow-up appointment, he asked us to sit down and, with a shaky hand, handed me a consent form for another surgery. I had, in fact, a Bellini tumor, a practically fatal kidney cancer. Nearly 100 percent of those afflicted with it do not survive.

My mother and her siblings had all died young, and, in my shocked state, I resigned myself to join them. Jordan and I drove home. We met our son on the street, and I told him that the news was very bad. I only had approximately ten months to live. The grief in his eyes was too much for me. It penetrated deep into my soul.

But something mysterious happened at the same time. Inexplicably, I felt my sins lifted from my shoulders, with the promise of new life to come. A profound peace filled my body. I was inspired to say, "The doctors have their professional opinion, but only God knows when I'm going to die." My worries, control, and oppressive self-pity were gone. This left me with a peaceful surrender to the will of God.

Within a few weeks I was back in the hospital. My friend, Queenie Yu, hearing I was sick, came to visit me with a care package. Among the gifts was an Asian depiction of the Madonna and Child, and a rosary blessed by Pope Francis. Queenie smiled her beautiful smile as I thanked her. She was surprised that I knew what a rosary was, although I didn't know how to pray it. My great-grandmother had been Catholic and, hearing that I was sick, a cousin of mine subsequently sent me her rosary. By that time it was probably over one hundred years old.

Queenie offered to teach me how to pray meditatively over the mysteries, coming daily to the hospital to pray with me. It often took us close to two hours to pray a set of mysteries, as I had much to say, much to pray for! She taught me to offer the Rosary for specific intentions, for individual people or particular needs. We prayed together like this for over a month. She explained the mysteries commemorated in each decade within the four sets of mysteries: the Joyful, Luminous, Sorrowful, and Glorious.

I told her stories of my family, relating how much I loved them, and reflected on how much I would miss them. I continued to practice prayer in this way for months, even after I left the hospital, and especially during periods when my illness intensified.

Constant scriptural prayer, embodied by the Rosary, saved me from worry and fear. I didn't let myself think about anything negative, not even self-pity. I prayed the Lord's Prayer throughout the long nights and the many uncomfortable scans. The prayers always saved me from fear, worry, and pain. I could see that my life was completely in God's hands and that my future wasn't up to me. I had lived my life for too long trying to control what is best surrendered into God's hands. I believe this trial of my illness was given to me to help me come to this realization.

My experience of God's goodness and the closeness of the Blessed Mother eventually brought me into the Catholic Church, at the Easter Vigil of 2024.

Now I start my day with God before I even open my eyes. Life's inevitable and ongoing challenges have inspired me to wear a large wooden-bead rosary with a sizeable bronze crucifix around my neck to bed. If I wake at night with any fear or worry, I hold on tight to the crucifix and ask Jesus to come to me. I always go right back to sleep. First thing in the morning I get dressed, put on my sneakers, wrap a light wooden-beaded rosary around my wrist, hold on to the crucifix, and head outdoors to walk a familiar way, praying as the sun rises. I reflect on the mysteries and the fruit of each decade. In the first decade I thank God for the amazing sunrise (a renewed and better directed "sun salutation"), and I thank him for giving me life for another day. In the second, third, and fourth decades I pray for whoever needs a prayer. In the fifth decade I ask God how I can do his will this day.

On the way back I listen to Scripture from the Holy Bible app. I have a verse of the day on my homepage that I can reflect on at any time. When I have challenges, I carry my small wooden rosary on my right wrist and hold the crucifix to remind me that I am a child of God. My meditation follows these prayers and continues throughout the day, as I listen for the Word of God, to discern the next right thing I can do. I have discovered the practical meaning of Psalm 119:105: "Thy word is a lamp to my feet and a light to my path."

I began this foreword speaking of focus, play, feeling grounded, and how I acquired tools early on to keep me in touch with myself and my surroundings. But nothing compares to knowing the Lord, who has become my true rock and the Savior of my life in more ways than one. He is my protection against the pain and uncertainty of this life.

Christian meditation is more than a practice, more than a tool for inner peace. It is a relationship with the living God. Like all good relationships, it develops out of vulnerability and trust. I thank God for the path he has placed me on and for the true wisdom he has given me through a share in the cross of his Son. I suppose nothing sharpens our focus as quickly as love or pain, and sometimes they are the same thing when we are called to sacrifice.

You will find these and other messages developed with depth and insight within the pages of Fr. John Henry's *The Fire and the Silence*. I met Fr. John Henry during my second visit to his monastery, St. Michael's Abbey, in Orange County, California. Jordan and I had dinner planned with them, followed by a speaking event in the plaza afterward. After having helicoptered in from Los Angeles, over the long stretches of Friday afternoon freeway traffic, Fr. John Henry escorted us to the church for Evening Prayer. He sat beside me and helped me with the prayer books. We also sat across from each other during the dinner in the special collections library.

During the event in the plaza I told the story of my conversion and the role prayer played in it. The next day Fr. John Henry and I began corresponding regarding prayers for Jordan's mother who was near death. We were able to meet in person again, this time backstage at an event in Thousand Oaks, in February 2025.

It is a joy for me to contribute a foreword to his book, which deeply resonates with my own journey in prayer and faith. The central point I draw from the pages that follow is one of love and desire that focus both mind and heart on God. As Father says, “The goal is not no-fire but a fire that burns for the Lord.” Fire and silence can go together. Our lives are truly defined by this fire from within, especially our interior life of union with the Lord.

Tammy M. Peterson
Paradise Valley, Arizona

AUTHOR'S PREFACE

In accepting Mike Aquilina's gracious invitation to write this book on how thoughts bear upon the life of prayer, I immediately thought of several things: New Testament injunctions to renew the mind in Christ, the patristic tradition of thoughts stretching back to the Egyptian deserts of the third and fourth centuries, and the helpful insights of modern psychology, particularly those found in the cognitive behavioral therapy of Aaron T. Beck. That's a lot to think about, and a lot to synthesize in a simple book intended for people who simply want to pray with fewer distractions.

I decided to craft the present volume not so much as a book of strategies for countering unhelpful thoughts, memories, and feelings, but rather as *lectio divina*, spiritual reading. That is, whatever strategies I do outline in these pages are always couched in a meditative framework, because to be perfectly up-front (spoiler alert), it is by consistently filling your mind with sacred concepts and prayerful reflection on them that you accomplish the reconquest of your mind for Christ. By reading this book you are already doing the very thing you want this book to help you accomplish.

Hence, we will reflect on biblical stories, patristic teachings, the wisdom of the saints, and the common sense of psychology to help us understand why we think the thoughts we think and how best to manage them. But the redemption of the mind is ultimately a work of grace; as such, it belongs to Christ. Prayerful reflection invites him into our inner world where his grace can heal, order, and make our thoughts fruitful.

Specialized volumes of a more therapeutic nature address particular areas of struggle, should your distractions result more from past trauma or some form of obsessiveness, for example. Although we restrict our concern here to wanderings amenable to spiritual self-discipline, it is important to underscore how Christ is the healer in either case. Whatever instrumentality he chooses is always up to him, and it is a mark of both gratitude and humility if we can receive all good things from him no matter what secondary causes he employs.

St. Teresa of Ávila, an authority on distraction and practically a coauthor of this book, heard Jesus tell her in prayer something comforting and encouraging for all who have ever tried to focus mind and heart in meditation. It will also help you manage and orient your expectations as you read the following pages.

Teresa recounts:

> On the vigil of St. Lawrence, just after receiving Communion, my mental faculties were so scattered and distracted I couldn't help myself, and I began to envy those who live in deserts and to think that since they don't hear or see anything they are free of this wandering of the mind. I heard: "You are greatly mistaken, daughter;

> rather, the temptations of the devil there are stronger; be patient, for as long as you live, a wandering mind cannot be avoided."[1]

In addition to Mike Aquilina, I wish to thank the entire staff at Scepter Publishers for their continued willingness to collaborate with me; I am grateful also (and always) to my religious superiors and the entire Norbertine community of St. Michael's Abbey for fraternal support and patience with me.

In a special way I would like to express my gratitude to Tammy Peterson and Dr. Jordan Peterson. Tammy's foreword reveals her as a faithful practitioner of interior prayer, which she learned firsthand in the midst of intense personal suffering. Dr. Jordan Peterson's influence is likewise in these pages; I respectfully cite him and thank him for inspiring a generation of young (and not so young) people to think about—and even to wrestle with—God.

ENDNOTES

1. Teresa of Ávila, *Spiritual Testimonies*, 39, in *The Collected Works of St. Teresa of Ávila*, vol. 1, trans. Kieran Kavanaugh and Otilio Rodriguez, rev. ed. (ICS, 1987), p. 409.

ONE
A Fire in the Head

I would love to claim Flannery O'Conner as the author of this introductory chapter by simply pasting without comment the following paragraph from her short story "A Temple of the Holy Ghost." The story depicts a young girl saying her prayers before bed, during which she

> took a running start and went through to the other side of the Apostle's Creed and then hung by her chin on the side of the bed, empty-minded. . . . Sometimes . . . she would be moved to fervor and would think of Christ on the long journey to Calvary, crushed three times under the rough cross. Her mind would stay on this a while and then get empty and when something roused her, she would find that she was thinking of a different thing entirely, of some dog or some girl or something she was going to do some day.[1]

Few authors better capture the pure randomness of the thought stream of someone at prayer, from the formal recitation of a prayer text to an empty mind drifting between images of the sacred and mundane… no further comment needed?

This book is written for people like O'Connor's character: people of prayer who experience the trials of inner disorder and need help navigating the chaos. On paper, the girl's disjointed thoughts raise a smile. Perhaps we go there every time we pray, and certainly we can relate to the apparent randomness of it all. But in the reality of our prayer life, distractions and wanderings of the mind can be a source of distress and discouragement. Clarity, likewise, regarding the moral culpability of our thoughts may be in question. Did I just consent to that bad thought? If so, to what extent? How can I tell? Scruples can torture the conscience with endless uncertainty.

Why isn't it easier, this battle for interior order, linear thoughts, and disciplined emotions? Why does imagination so easily dominate the interior life? Why do memories return unbidden and distract if not torment the well-meaning mind? How is it that a meditation on the passion and death of the Lord can, by almost imperceptible micro-steps, devolve into rumination on, I don't know, some movie we saw twenty years ago?

Thoughts as wanted or unwanted may be relative to one's state of soul. For most readers, I would imagine, a thought classified as unwanted is one incompatible with our spiritual and moral goals. Because those goals align with what is truly good for human nature and Christian spiritual life, the thoughts appear as more or less obvious deviations. Where goals do not match with the good of nature or of Christian spirituality, things get more complicated. Unwanted in this context may be just the thing we need, like Saul on the way to Damascus. The more unwanted the better, if the thoughts are of Jesus, repentance, and forgiveness. Parker, Flannery O'Connor's protagonist in "Parker's Back," finds this inner disturbance in a tattoo parlor, where a Byzantine icon of Christ captures his attention and prompts him to demand that the tattooist trace and ink it onto his back. The discomfort caused in one who is not pursuing godly goals, not trying to live a holy and meaningful life, is very good.

What Jesus does in the Gospels when he interrupts people's lives to call or challenge them is often initially unwanted. Simon Peter does not want to go fishing again after a night of empty nets and no sleep. The same kind of thing happens whenever the Lord begins to whisper in the ear of someone who is not particularly close to him and has no intention of being. Many conversions have transpired in the souls of people who were not looking for conversion but who found everything they could ever want in the love of Jesus—because he disrupted their expected thoughts and routine desires. "I didn't think God would get hold of me the way he did, either. But, let me tell you once again: God doesn't ask our permission to *complicate* our lives. He just gets in: and that's that!"[2]

Once we are set firmly on the narrow road that leads to the kingdom, then sustained effort is needed so that we don't fall back into old ways of thinking. Temptations return. Unhelpful old friends reemerge. Bad habits are easy to fall back into. But whether we continue on the right path or are tempted to step back onto the old, everything begins with our thoughts.

Although the role of thoughts in the interior life of prayer is our main focus, thoughts cannot be considered in isolation from other facets of life, whether intellectual, affective, or spiritual. Psychological strategies may be effectively employed in controlling our thoughts, discerning and understanding them, and testing them against reality. These can provide relief from inner distress, as well as clarifying our perceptions, which is no small feat. But prayer is not all about concentration and control of our interior states. Before all else it is a response to grace, a surrender, a fact we will not tire of repeating. Thoughts are only one aspect of our spiritual life—an extremely important aspect—but they cannot be divorced from the larger framework of morals, habits, goals, and what we want to get out of prayer in the first place.

Prayer is God's initiative. Prayer is not an activity we just decide to do at random. If "no one can say 'Jesus is Lord' except by the Holy Spirit" (1 Cor 12:3), we might also conclude that the same Holy Spirit inspires all authentic prayer, as St. Paul seems to say: "for we do not know how to pray as we ought, but the Spirit himself intercedes for us with sighs too deep for words" (Rom 8:26). How our thoughts factor into God's initiative, invitation, and inspiration cannot be ignored. In the process of learning what our thoughts mean, why they go where they go, why they recur, where they come from, we learn at the same time what it means for the Lord to be our healer, our love, our truth, our life, our Redeemer.

Thus our promise here is not that by the last page you will possess techniques to keep your memory and imagination from wandering ever again. Wandering is not so much the problem; we will see that, as your own experience teaches you, it is ineluctable. We have already heard St. Teresa recount the Lord's assurance of its inevitability. But inevitable does not mean unmanageable. Nor does inevitable mean that progress in interior order and inner quiet is an unrealizable goal. Improvement is truly possible if we keep in mind the relative scale of growth, which will always be more or less impaired by the consequences of our fallen nature.

One of the great monastic fathers of the Egyptian desert, St. Moses (ca. 400), commented centuries ago: "It is impossible for the mind not to be approached by thoughts, but it is in the power of every earnest man either to admit them or to reject them."[3] A degree of chaos is implied, to be sure, but an even higher degree of personal freedom is assured. The challenge is attaining strength and consistency in that level of freedom.

If any promise is made here, it is that of another early monastic father from the same Egyptian desert, St. Nesteros (ca. 400), who assures us that as the fruit of wise, prudent, and consistent interior struggle, "it will come to pass that not only every purpose and thought of your heart, but also all the wanderings and rovings of your imagination will become to you a holy and unceasing pondering of the Divine law."[4]

You might think that the only time your every intention, thought, desire, and imagination are so centered on something is when you are . . . in love? worried? frightened? You would be right, and that is very instructive. Strong desires, powerful emotions focus the mind like nothing else. The obvious conclusion is that not only strong but ordered desires and their corresponding emotions "will keep your hearts and your minds in Christ Jesus" (Phil 4:7), because as the same verse tells us, order reflects "the peace of God, which passes all understanding."

We will return to his important guidance in a later chapter. For now, know that this is very possible, but be more aware that grace and not methodology will take us there. The order of grace is the order of gifts. It is the order of the possible in the midst of the humanly impossible. What makes a virgin to be with child, what raises the dead, what heals the sick and dying is the same power we have available to us.

Some final words about the unusual epigraph. The Aengus of W. B. Yeats's poem, a figure from Irish lore, still wanders in search of a magical girl in the poet's rendition of the tale, implying an endless journey for love that paradoxically does not disappoint. Echoes of Wisdom's praise of herself resound here: "Those who eat me will hunger for more, and those who drink me will thirst for more" (Sir 24:21). Union of lover and beloved occurs, according to the myth, yet only after Aengus transforms himself into a swan, to match the form the girl herself has taken.

Our goal is not a mind completely at rest but one directed and driven toward the good that is God. In that directionality is the best kind of rest: We are no longer aiming at nothing, and so meandering everywhere, but intentional about where we're going. The bride of the Canticle of Canticles rests but little in her pursuit of the mysterious, uncanny bridegroom. She too has a fire in her head, and especially in her heart. The goal is not no-fire but a fire that burns for the Lord.

We are made to love and so cannot help pursing the things we love. "Every human being must love or go crazy," says Bl. Fulton Sheen. "Direct love toward God, and peace comes over the soul: turn it from God, and the heart becomes a broken fountain where tears fall."[5]

Heart and treasure are always aligned, but the quality of our treasure measures the quality of our hearts, of our love. If Jesus censures "the hypocrites" for loving to be seen praying in public, and the Pharisees for loving places and marks of honor (Mt 6:5; 23:6), it is more a criticism of their hearts than the actual fact of being seen and having a prominent seat. The dubious reward you get for loving these things is the fleeting things themselves.

You have come to these pages, in any case, because something like a fire stirs in your mind—and at times and places you might rather it didn't. But like wildfires, containment and redirection are important strategic elements of the solution. Extinguishing the blaze altogether is the endgame, of course, where fires are destructive. But where flames may serve a purpose, as in a controlled burn, they can be tolerated within safe limits. The idea of the counterfire that deprives an oncoming fire of combustible brush may be even more apt. One of the most powerful biblical analogies for transformation is this: "I came to cast fire upon the earth; and would that it were already kindled" (Lk 12:49)!

If you are troubled by unwanted thoughts, it is because there are thoughts you do want and you would like a little more control over the former so that the latter can flourish unhindered. Helpful biblical images of men on journeys waylaid or obstructed by adversaries include the parable of the Good Samaritan (Lk 10:30–37), wherein the ambushed traveler is restored to health by a stranger's mercy, and going back much further, the episode of David and his men harassed by Shimei's peltering with rocks, dirt, and insults (2 Sam 16:5–14). David, too, was refreshed at the end of that journey, at the river Jordan.

The point of these examples is that the seemingly thankless struggle between a journey hallowed by God's blessing and the more or less frequent ambush of thoughts bent on diverting us is something God at least permits to mature us, to teach us something valuable about his mercy and strength. Only through struggle and fidelity do we grow, and sometimes the adversary needs to present formidable interference so that our growth may increase proportionately.

Prayer is not for the fainthearted. Prayer is the ultimate transformative act. As we unite with God he will not leave us unchanged but will call us to die to self, to alter our course, to say or do what never occurred to us before. All of this so that we might actually live in love and freedom, possessing the full joy that is Christ's own, which he prays we may share with him without fear of loss (see Jn 16:22; 17:13).

Indeed, a voice we will continue to hear many times in these pages, that of our coauthor St. Teresa of Ávila, insists that we must begin this journey of prayer by cultivating freedom and joy, so as not to think all is lost should distractions pester us: "Now strive in the beginning to walk in joy and freedom, for there are some persons who think their devotion will go away if they become a little distracted."[6] I want to insert this here to set the tone for the rest of the book, and to set the reader at rest. Recognize that your slightest attempt to pray is pleasing to God beyond imagining. Your heavenly Father loves to hear from you and is not constantly judging you for the inevitable flights of mind consequent upon our fallen nature.

We come to prayer not to change God but to let him change us. More and more we allow him the freedom to transform all that is fallen in us by healing the places broken by fear, distrust, self-loathing, and all that prevents our joy from being as full as it can be.

As Aengus transformed himself to remain ever with his beloved, we will find a transformation demanded of us, if we would stay always with our beloved Lord, at least in thought and desire. It is what St. Paul exhorts and what we need to clear the path for: "Do not be conformed to this world but be transformed by the renewal of your mind, that you may prove what is the will of God, what is good and acceptable and perfect" (Rom 12:2).

ENDNOTES

1. Flannery O'Connor, "A Temple of the Holy Ghost," in *The Complete Stories* (Farrar, Straus and Giroux, 1971), p. 244.

2. Josemaría Escrivá, *The Forge* (Scepter, 2002), no. 902.

3. John Cassian, "First Conference of Abbot Moses," in *The Conferences of John Cassian*, vol. 11 of *A Select Library of Nicene and Post-Nicene Fathers of the Christian Church*, Second Series, ed. Philip Schaff and Henry Wace, trans. C. S. Gibson (Buffalo, NY: Christian Literature, 1894), p. 303, accessed at https://www.newadvent.org/fathers/350801.htm.

4. John Cassian, "The First Conference of Abbot Nesteros," in *Nicene and Post-Nicene Fathers*, Second Series, vol. 11, p. 442, accessed at www.newadvent.org.

5. Fulton J. Sheen, *Peace of Soul* (Whittlesey House, 1949), pp. 29–30.

6. Teresa of Ávila, *The Book of Her Life*, in *The Collected Works of St. Teresa of Ávila*, vol. 1, p. 123.

CHAPTER TWO
Confessions & Possibilities

I will never forget a young man I met years ago who thought that chastity was basically impossible. It was an unquestioned assumption based on the combined strength of inveterate habits and the recurring thoughts and temptations they would incite. I want to take a red Sharpie and really underscore, circle, and scribble frantic arrows around this: *He didn't even question it.* It was a tacit assumption, a given, call it what you will. It was not open to discussion.

Compounding the difficulty was his own contribution to the problem: He had repeatedly chosen to consume obscene materials, so that added to his vice was the shame of a self-inflicted predicament. He had aggravated the problem and could not deliver himself from it.

Then he read St. Augustine's *Confessions.*

If you have not yet discovered this fourth-century account of the saint's journey to orthodox Christianity in tandem with his moral conversion from an unchaste life, allow me to invite you to "take up and read; take up and read."[1]

The Confessions is not even primarily about a man's struggle to break free from habits of impurity, but the dramatic tension that accompanies Augustine's conversion speaks—for all time, in the most powerful way—to everyone who has ever experienced the enslaving power of vice and the desire to be free. The agony of renouncing powerful pleasures of the world and the flesh before even greater joys of the spirit, however, is a true struggle that can leave us feeling defeated and hopeless. The high ideal is enthroned before us; but ambivalence, futility, and fear raise formidable doubts within.

Augustine himself weeps, tears his hair, doubles over, and pounds his forehead—all in the midst of his anguish to reject the habits that held him bound, so as to live in the freedom of the children of God. That is the visible graphic of the essentially internal conflict between *yes* and *no*, between *never again* and *just one more time*. Yet at the tipping point, he discovers in the Word of God the grace of possibility. After reading Romans 13:13–14, he asserts that he had no need to read more; all was clear:

> . . . let us conduct ourselves becomingly as in the day, not in reveling and drunkenness, not in debauchery and licentiousness, not in quarreling and jealousy. But put on the Lord Jesus Christ, and make no provision for the flesh, to gratify its desires.

The young man whom I mentioned saw himself and his own struggles reflected on so many pages of this masterpiece that he finally uttered the golden word: *possible.*

It brings to mind the very last page of Dostoevsky's classic *Crime and Punishment*, where the intractable Raskolnikov, serving his prison sentence in Siberia, finally considers the possibility of conversion. Holding the still unopened Bible given him by Sonia, the woman who has thanklessly but indefatigably loved him, the narrative recounts that "one thought passed through his mind: 'Can her convictions not be mine now? Her feelings, her aspirations at least. . . .'"[2] Change of mind and conversion of heart are not easier than a camel's passage through the needle's eye, but "what is impossible with men is possible with God" (Lk 18:27).

Possibility is a saving word for those who have walked through the valley of the shadow of death or who sit in darkness and chains. Possibility means hope, and hope leads ultimately to God. But where every avenue seems closed and every door locked, we need to know that God has ways of saving us that lie outside our minds altogether. We cannot imagine them. If salvation history teaches us anything, it is that God's ways regularly violate the limits we insist on imposing on both nature and grace.

An early chapter on struggle and possibility is crucial. The discouragement easily felt in our interior life makes the unwanted thought project seem impossible, like trying to keep out ants or flies in the summer: One always gets in, and likely more than one. Or it's like a game of whack-a-mole, or beheading the hydra: One intense gesture does not suffice for global and final conquest. Or, again, from a literary point of view, with the distinctively (and appropriately) complicated syntax of Gerard Manley Hopkins's poem: "let me . . . not live this tormented mind / With this tormented mind tormenting yet."[3] In other words, there seems no way out, especially when the mind itself is inescapable.

The human brain is the most complex thing in the created order; its processes must be respected. Hence our ideal is not to create a mental vacuum into which thoughts may only enter by permission. The mind is not such an airtight vessel, as frustrating as that might seem, yet better that it not be. A closed mind is generally no improvement over a mind perpetually open. The point is to know when to keep it open and when to close it. Chesterton's common sense regarding the "fallacy of the open mind" rings true here: "An open mind is really a mark of foolishness, like an open mouth. Mouths and minds were made to shut; they were made to open only in order to shut."[4]

From this, a healthy sense of humor about the whole thing is indicated. Prayer is serious business. Yet the great St. Teresa says it is quite natural for its practitioners to laugh "as at a fool when this intellect—or mind, to explain myself better—goes off to the more foolish things of the world."[5] That willingness to laugh at ourselves is both a sign and means to humility, without which it is difficult to call any words we say to God "prayer." As proof, check in with the tax collector in the outer courts of the temple.

This fluid and sometimes chaotic place we call the mind can be made into a venue for healing and redemption as we "take every thought captive to obey Christ" (2 Cor 10:5). We want Jesus at the center of our thoughts and affections so that he can help us discern the bad and hold fast to the good, somewhat like the dragnet image to which he compares the kingdom of God: “When it was full, men drew it ashore and sat down and sorted the good into vessels but threw away the bad” (Mt 13:48).

If you are willing at this point to accept that with God all things are possible, even what you may assume is impossible in your particularly difficult life, then you have more than enough hope to sustain you for the journey ahead. The only irremediable mistake is to quit. God can work with our mistakes, our stupidity, our failures, so long as we are willing to keep trying.

ENDNOTES

1. For the famous allusion, see Augustine, *Confessions*, 8.12, trans. R. S. Pine-Coffin (Penguin Books, 1961).

2. Fyodor Dostoyevsky, *Crime and Punishment*, trans. Constance Garnett (The Modern Library, 1950), p. 515.

3. Gerard Manley Hopkins, “My own heart let me more have pity on,” in *Poems of Gerard Manley Hopkins*, ed. Robert Bridges (Humphrey Milford, 1918) p. 67.

4. G. K. Chesterton, “The History of Religions,” for *The Illustrated London News* (September 26, 1908): https://library.chesterton.org/the-history-of-religions-71991/.

5. Teresa of Ávila, *The Way of Perfection,* in *The Collected Works of St. Teresa of Ávila*, vol. 2, trans. Kieran Kavanaugh and Otilio Rodriguez (ICS, 1980), p. 158.

THREE
Listening to Spies

Speaking of possible, the account of Joshua, Caleb, and the spies sent by Moses to scout out the Promised Land needs space here. I am certainly not the first to compare the Land and its fearsome inhabitants to our interior landscape of thoughts and feelings.

Ancient and longstanding tradition in biblical exegesis allegorically interprets the as-yet unconquered and unsettled land of Canaan: It is a symbol of the soul, occupied by numerous and intimidating forces, fearsome to behold and seemingly impossible to overcome. The Canaanite tribes are often referred to allegorically as faults, vices, passions, or simply as "thoughts," as in the *Conferences* of St. John Cassian, the seminal fifth-century collection of discourses from the elders of the Egyptian desert: namely gluttony, fornication (or lust), avarice, anger, dejection, acedia (or listlessness), vainglory, and pride.[1] It is from these spirits or faults that our troublesome thoughts arise.

Some commentators discern an order to the thoughts, or passions, such that one leads to another. Perhaps not easy to see in all cases, at least the connection between gluttony and fornication (or excess in food and drink precipitating lust) is plain enough. What is very clear is that vices do not grow or act alone, just as virtues do not develop independent of one another, unlike muscle groups. Hence to grow in one virtue helps all the others to increase, as repetition of vice invites other types of moral corruption as well.

Numbers 13 recounts the reconnoitering of the land carried out by spies, appointed representatives of the twelve tribes, among whom were Joshua and Caleb. The report is mixed. Those sent to spy out the land find that it is indeed rich and fruitful, but inhabited by impossible adversaries. The inhabitants are like giants, they say, beside whom they felt as small as grasshoppers.

The people are dismayed at the report, yet Joshua and Caleb insist that conquest is possible (remember that word?)—possible because it is willed by God. But their testimony avails little; a riot of sorts ensues. The people's dismay quickly becomes discouragement that snowballs into an open rebellion. Their doubting rendered the people unfit for passage into the land God wanted to give them.

> Who were they that heard and yet were rebellious? Was it not all those who left Egypt under the leadership of Moses? And with whom was he provoked forty years? Was it not with those who sinned, whose bodies fell in the wilderness? And to whom did he swear that they should never enter his rest, but to those who were disobedient?

So we see that they were unable to enter because of unbelief. (Heb 3:16–19)

Apart from the intimidation factor that dismayed the Israelites, also noteworthy was the cultural factor. God would lead them into a rich but not trouble-free land, not a place devoid of trial and temptation. If even Adam and Eve required a test of their freedom in Paradise—a sign that God respects the dignity of his rational creatures—then the Israelites could not expect a land more idyllic than Paradise itself. Especially after the fall of our first parents do we need struggle and sacrifice to regain personal integrity.

The land of Canaan, so named after the apparently illegitimate grandson of Noah,[2] would be a foreseen moral danger for the chosen people, at least until they could subdue it. Leviticus 19 catalogs the largely sexual deviancies that God needed to warn his people about not involving themselves in. As these practices were widespread, culturally accepted, and sometimes religiously sanctioned (such as cultic prostitution), the pressure to assimilate would be intense. It takes little imagination to connect the dots with our contemporary culture, with the ubiquitous depersonalization of human sexuality, frequent exposure to obscenity, and the pressure to accept it all as normal.

What you would never think of doing when removed from tempting circumstances may prove to be almost irresistible when immersed in conditions that make it easy and an almost necessary means of fitting in. "Everyone does it" is a far subtler and more compelling pressure than we give it credit for, as much for adults as for children. G. K. Chesterton devastatingly comments that when people begin consorting with demons along the lines of the cultic worship practiced by the Canaanite tribes, then “Sooner or later a man deliberately sets himself to do the most disgusting thing he can think of.”[3] Leviticus 19 is a catalog of those very things.

God was knowingly bringing his people into a land both fearsome and potentially seductive and corruptive. Why? To conquer and convert it. It would take an in-depth Bible study to unpack the divine plan for both the people and the land in the context of salvation history. That the Holy Land was intended to be Shem’s inheritance and not that of Canaan, the usurper, enjoys a longstanding place in the interpretative history of the Old Testament (see Gn 9:24–27). For our purposes we should see the pattern set for ourselves. God, likewise knowingly, brings us into a fallen world with evident threats, seductions, and corrupting influences. Why? To conquer and convert it—beginning, however, with the most hidden parts of ourselves: our thoughts and affections.

The story of the spies reflects the fraught landscape of our thought life. We too are called to live in a world where scandals and temptations “are sure to come” (Lk 17:1), where dovelike innocence and serpentine craftiness are demanded. But we need to know what may no longer be obvious: It is possible to conquer ourselves and convert more deeply to the Lord, even as the world appears to fall further and further from God. It is possible to achieve a relative but significant order, an integration, in our interior life. Vaguely “trying” or “concentrating” harder, however, is not the strategy. We have a battle to fight, but the victory will go to those who can accept this word: “The Lord will fight for you, and you have only to be still”

(Ex 14:14). That's not the kind of fighting we're used to, so we must learn how to fight with borrowed strength.

Joshua and Caleb weren't blind. They saw all the same sights as the other ten spies. The difference was in their trust. They believed not that they were stronger than the inhabitants of the land, but that God would enable them to do whatever he commanded. Yet their attempts to quell the fears of the people were to no avail.

> And Joshua the son of Nun and Caleb the son of Jephun'neh, who were among those who had spied out the land, rent their clothes, and said to all the congregation of the people of Israel, "The land, which we passed through to spy it out, is an exceedingly good land. If the Lord delights in us, he will bring us into this land and give it to us, a land which flows with milk and honey. Only, do not rebel against the Lord; and do not fear the people of the land, for they are bread for us; their protection is removed from them, and the Lord is with us; do not fear them." But all the congregation said to stone them with stones. (Nm 14:6–10)

The people thought the whole thing was a setup. They thought Joshua and Caleb were giving an overly optimistic pep talk, at the end of which they would be slain before they could barely set foot in this supposedly fertile and productive land.

The importance of this episode is not only to underscore the need to trust in God for possibilities that exceed our strength. I have included this story to show how we can waste mental or imaginative space worrying about whether God is with us or not, whether we are loved or not, whether providence guides our lives or not. Thoughts of being abandoned, unloved, unseen, and uncared for are certainly high on the list of unwanted thoughts. We will not be able to dismiss them easily, or at all, unless we are assured that the Lord is with us, even in the hidden places of mind and heart.

Benedict XVI, years before his pontificate, got very real about these lingering, pestering doubts, and laid them out as a series of existential questions:

> We come now to the all-important question: Is it true, then, when someone says to me: "It is good that you exist"? Is it really good? Is it not possible that that person's love, which wills my existence, is just a tragic error? If the love that gives me courage to exist is not based on truth, then I must, in the end, come to curse the love that deceives me, that maintains in existence something that were better destroyed. . . . Even without such evidence, it is obvious, however, that the apparently so simple act of liking myself, of being at one with myself, actually raises the question of the whole universe. It raises the question of truth: Is it good that I exist? Is it good that anything at all exists? Is the world good? How many persons today would dare to affirm this question from the heart—to believe it is good that they exist? That is the source of the anxiety and despair that incessantly affect mankind. Love alone is of no avail. It serves no purpose if truth is not on its side. Only when truth and love are in harmony can man know joy. For it is truth that makes man free.[4]

It will do us no good to deal with frequently recurring thoughts—like the hopelessness and rage displayed in the story of the spies—without identifying the underlying attitude that gives birth to them. A feeling of lovelessness, whether attributed to human relationships or to our relationship with God, cannot continue to loiter in the background of our prayer life. God addressed the Israelites through Moses with the basis for trust in him: "You have seen what I did to the Egyptians, and how I bore you on eagles' wings and brought you to myself" (Ex 19:4). Right. Read the soteriological room: Read the plagues, read the Red Sea, read the desert of Sinai. What does it all tell you?

The Exodus generation had seen things that no one had ever seen before, or since: the dramatic spectacle of the plagues, the Passover, the crossing of the Red Sea. What they saw coming out of Egypt was the very cost of their own salvation. All these Egyptians died that the people of God might live. And yet, at the crucial moment of their entrance into the Promised Land, they would not trust the testimony of Joshua and Caleb, nor could they bring themselves to trust that God would bring them in safely and defeat their enemies for them. So they did not enter into what God calls his "rest" (Ps 95:11).

The rest or peace of mind we are seeking is costly. Trust in God's saving and healing power demands wholehearted faith, a faith that can look retrospectively and prospectively at the mercies of the past and the hope of future promises.

A very important postscript to this is that nothing about our spiritual life will be healthy without a firm and growing conviction of God's love for us. Basically, this issue needs resolution as you continue your journey with the Lord. I almost said "before" you can get anywhere spiritually, before continuing your journey, this needs to be rock solid. But no demand is made here that you have the question perfectly resolved. As far as your other relationships go, you might suffer from feeling unloved and/or unlovable much of the time. This might be an additional obstacle with roots deep in childhood.

Healing-in-progress, however, is not an impediment to spiritual growth. It accompanies it, inevitably. Healing cannot, however, be hurried by someone else's enthusiasm. When we speak of God's personal love for each one of us, we are not depending on enthusiasm, nor about leaning on other people's experiences of divine love. These help. They are there to help, so we should pay close attention to the testimonies of changed people. Ultimately, however, the question is a personal one and needs to be answered by you and only you. You cannot leave it unaddressed and continue doing spiritual things and expect deep transformation.

Fine. So what do you do? I normally recommend that people put themselves in a position where God can speak to them. Since we are most accustomed to communicating verbally, although this is far from the only mode of communication, then take up the Word of God in a prayerful, reflective way. Read those passages that especially speak of God's love for you. Read them slowly and repeatedly. Ask why God is speaking in this way. Ask why he wants you to hear him speaking in this way. Let the Word penetrate you. Remember that the inspired Word of God is unlike any other book; the words have a sacramental quality that touch and heal the soul. If you can manage to practice this meditative reading before the Blessed Sacrament, then you will be in the presence of him who, after all, dwells among us in the Eucharist as a reminder of his total love for us.

If God is the life of the soul, if he dwells continually at the center of the soul, then we cannot avoid reckoning with this presence that literally keeps us together, keeps us whole, and still call our spiritual life a "life." Even those in mortal sin retain his sustaining presence, as St. John of the Cross says, so that "It brings special happiness to a person to understand that God is never absent, not even from a soul in mortal sin."[5] That level of unshakable closeness and intimate companionship has startled many saints into looking within for the Lord, and they have truly discovered that the kingdom of God is within.

We can distract ourselves or stay on the surface, but the depths continually cry out with a song of divine love, trying to get our attention, trying to convince us that we can trust him enough to enter the depths and find him. Your own inner Canaan needs conquest, and you can trust the Lord to sustain you in whatever fight you have to face. You cannot face it alone, and he does not want you to. One of my favorite contemporary sayings is perfect here: *Your mind is like a bad neighborhood: Don't go in alone.*

St. Alphonsus Ligouri (1696–1787) cites a passage attributed to St. Thomas Aquinas which, although spurious, Liguori quotes with full approval: "God loves man just as if man were his god, and as if without man he could not be happy; as if man were the god of God himself, and without him he could not be happy."[6] Give such sentiments ample mental space; let your imagination ponder and play with them. Read them while looking at the crucifix. Be driven to distraction by them. And then think how this exchange between the Lover and Beloved in the Song of Songs reflects God's attitude toward you:

> The voice of my beloved!
>   Behold, he comes,
> leaping upon the mountains,
>   bounding over the hills.
> My beloved is like a gazelle,
>   or a young stag.
> Behold, there he stands
>   behind our wall,
> gazing in at the windows,
>   looking through the lattice.
> My beloved speaks and says to me:
> "Arise, my love, my fair one,
>   and come away;
> for lo, the winter is past,
>   the rain is over and gone.
> The flowers appear on the earth,
>   the time of singing has come,
> and the voice of the turtledove
>   is heard in our land.
> The fig tree puts forth its figs,
>   and the vines are in blossom;
>   they give forth fragrance.
> Arise, my love, my fair one,
>   and come away.

> O my dove, in the clefts of the rock,
> in the covert of the cliff,
> let me see your face,
> let me hear your voice,
> for your voice is sweet,
> and your face is comely. (Song 2:8–14)

God has nothing better to do with his love than pour it out on you. If that's hard to believe, it is at least consistent with how he acts.

Ratzinger's conclusion above, that truth and love must go together unless we would lose joy altogether and consider love a farce, finds in the gospel the only possible solution. It is the radical response of God becoming man in Christ, and Christ demonstrating our worth by laying himself down on the Cross in testimony:

> The content of the Christian *evangelium* reads: God finds man so important that he himself has suffered for man. The Cross, which was for Nietzsche the most detestable expression of the negative character of the Christian religion, is in truth the center of the *evangelium*, the glad tidings: "It is good that you exist"—no, "It is necessary that you exist." The Cross is the approbation of our existence, not in words, but in an act so completely radical that it caused God to become flesh and pierced this flesh to the quick; that, to God, it was worth the death of his incarnate Son. One who is so loved that the other identifies his life with this love and no longer desires to live if he is deprived of it; one who is loved even unto death—such a

one knows that he is truly loved. But if God so loves us, then we are loved in truth. Then love is truth, and truth is love. Then life is worth living. This is the *evangelium*. This is why, even as the message of the Cross, it is glad tidings for one who believes; the only glad tidings that destroy the ambiguity of all other joys and make them worthy to be joy.[7]

ENDNOTES

1. See John Cassian, *Conference of Abbot Serapion on the Eight Principal Faults*.

2. Gn 9:20–27. Some interpreters see the sin of Ham as an attempt to usurp his father's authority by an act of maternal incest, thus spawning Canaan. See John Sietze Bergsma and Scott Walker Hahn, "Noah's Nakedness and the Curse on Canaan (Gn 9:20–27)," Journal of Biblical Literature 124, no. 1 (2005), pp. 25–40. https://doi.org/10.2307/30040989 * https://www.jstor.org/stable/30040989.

3. G. K. Chesterton, *The Everlasting Man* (Dodd, Mead, 1925), p. 133.

4. Joseph Ratzinger, *Principles of Catholic Theology: Building Stones for a Fundamental Theology*, trans. Mary Francis McCarthy (Ignatius Press, 1987), p. 80. Thanks to Fr. Conor Sullivan and Sr. Miriam James Heidland, SOLT, for the reference.

5. John of the Cross, *The Spiritual Canticle*, stanza 1.8, in *The Collected Works of St. John of the Cross*, trans. Kieran Kavanaugh and Otilio Rodriguez, rev. ed. (ICS, 1991), p. 480. To clarify further St. John's teaching here, which simply restates a truth of Catholic theology, it may be helpful to read it in conjunction with the CCC no. 308 and no. 1895. The type of presence in the soul

spoken of by St. John is a sustaining presence, without which no creature can exist. He is not speaking of the presence of grace or of charity, which mortal sin strikes from the soul, and which can ordinarily be restored only through sacramental confession. For a deeper look into the modes of God's presence in the created order see Thomas Aquinas, *Summa Theologiae*, I.8.

6. Alphonsus Liguori, *The Incarnation, Birth and Infancy of Jesus Christ* (Redemptorist Fathers, 1927), p. 15.

7. Ratzinger, *Principles of Catholic Theology*, p. 81.

FOUR

Why Your Mind Doesn't Work

G. K. Chesterton once expressed bemusement over the fact that some who are skeptical of religion in general and Christianity in particular could deny the reality of original sin. He claims somewhat facetiously that it is the only doctrine that can be proved empirically. "You can see it in the street," he says.[1]

I'm not sure if anyone reading this book needs a catechesis on original sin (that is, on the fact that human beings are conceived in a state of inherited sin and live with the effects of sin throughout life). You won't find anything approaching a complete exposition here, but the teaching is far from irrelevant for the subject at hand. A significant part of the answer to why our minds do not work, at least not with a programmable reliability like a computer, is that a fundamental discord sounds continually in the soul. The disruption of the original harmony in the human soul consequent upon the original sin leaves us prone to gravitate downward to base desires. Something so deeply ingrained is bound to affect how we think, pray, love, pretty much everything.

Psychologists Miller and Rollnick, authors of the bestselling *Motivational Interviewing*, speak of human ambivalence in decision-making as a sign of something foundationally wrong. As social psychologists, they avoid the language of sin while indirectly confirming Chesterton's point. When trying to stop doing things difficult to stop doing (for example, drinking, smoking, unhealthy eating),

> other motives conflict with doing the right thing, even when you know what it is. Ambivalence is simultaneously wanting and not wanting something, or wanting both of two incompatible things. It has been human nature since the dawn of time.[2]

Indeed it has. Wanting to obey God, wanting to live in paradise, but also wanting something forbidden as though you were missing out, as though the best thing was being withheld from you by a tyrant. These are some of the ambivalences of original sin, which clearly have everything to do with our tainted way of thinking. It echoes Elijah's ultimatum to the people of Israel on Mount Carmel, when he warned them to choose between the true God and the false god Ba'al (see 1 Kgs 18). Although outwardly they reverenced the Lord, the people sometimes tapped Ba'al as a backchannel to get things like fertility, wealth, or power, in a quality or quantity that God might not have willed for them. It is a spiritual black market that has never closed, since the dawn of time.

Original sin begets in us the strange but real temptation to throw away everything we value, to betray our sacred promises, to sever or weaken the ties of kinship, to sacrifice reputation and status, and especially to turn away from God like we don't know him, all for the sake of a single moment of self-preservation or sinful gratification. It was found in David's lust for Bathsheba; it was found in the betrayals of Judas Iscariot and St. Peter; it is found in you and me, either latent or active. We are capable of the worst. If we have not done the worst we are capable of, it is only by the grace of God. This is why the saying "There but for the grace of God go I" is more than a cliché. With even rudimentary self-knowledge, we can guess with some accuracy where we might be if God were not protecting us. Adam and Eve threw away everything in a moment, and they had everything they could want. Yet the mystery of mercy is that God was there to retrieve them from complete loss and even use their failure as the precursor to the coming of the Savior.

Those who find it a stretch to trace our common problem back to one man and one woman, a father and mother, may have no hesitation tracing other personal problems to their birth parents or upbringing. In both cases there is truth. However, we must take care not to identify either the devil or our parents in the suspect lineup every time we act badly. Adam blamed Eve (and God indirectly); Eve blamed the serpent. But the truth was in their choice to turn away from God, and it is this metaphysical avoidant behavior that they have bequeathed to us.

Universal redemption in Christ, incarnate of the Virgin Mary, is predicated on the inherited consequences of this fall. It is St. Paul's teaching that "as in Adam all die, so also in Christ shall all be made alive" (1 Cor 15:22).

> For if many died through one man's trespass, much more have the grace of God and the free gift in the grace of that one man Jesus Christ abounded for many. . . . If, because of one man's trespass, death reigned through that one man, much more will those who receive the abundance of grace and the free gift of righteousness reign in life through the one man Jesus Christ.
>
> Then as one man's trespass led to condemnation for all men, so one man's act of righteousness leads to acquittal and life for all men. For as by one man's disobedience many were made sinners, so by one man's obedience many will be made righteous. (Rom 5:15, 17–19)

The idea that something so terrible, so awful, at the origins of the human race could have left a moral mark on all of us may sound too simplistic against the evident complexity of the world, but the fact that nothing manmade can remediate it—no humanly devised therapeutics, for instance—except the terrible and awful suffering of the Son of God, should at least make us think twice about dismissing the disease along with the cure, especially a cure that cost the second Adam his life. In the context of discussing original sin, St. Thomas Aquinas cites John the Baptist's prophetic cry as indicating the one and only remedy: "'Behold the Lamb of God, behold him Who taketh away the sin of the world': and the reason for the employment of the singular is that the 'sin of the world' is original sin."[3]

As a consistent proof against skepticism we have the saints. Whenever we encounter them, we meet people who have taken the gospel very seriously by letting it reroute their entire lives. Even more to our point, we do in fact meet healed people—integrated people, whose love is ordered and ardent. They are initially as broken as any of us, yet by opening themselves to grace in a radical way, they literally let God heal them from the roots up. This is not to imply complete freedom from sin, nor complete absence of flaws and failures, but to assert that significant healing of the soul is both possible and willed by God, so that where our thoughts stray, they yet lack the power to dictate how we act. Acting out of wounds, acting out of fallen desires, is what grace and growth in virtue help us to avoid.

A sure sign that we are growing both spiritually and affectively is the decrease in our proclivity to act out of our woundedness. From a motivational default setting, our wounds become less and less a source of action/reaction. Although always present to some degree, their power to dominate thinking and acting is replaced by a graced growth in virtue.

This is important because although everyone knows something is fundamentally wrong with us, not everyone knows what's right about us. Neither can be ignored without detriment to the other. Saints bring the contrast into high relief. Saints show us, as veritable trophies of God's power, what human beings can be like at their best.

Disagreement over how to measure what makes a human being a "good" human being can range from personal and social functionality to the flourishing born of virtue and grace endorsed by Catholic theology and anthropology. Which camp you fall into is not completely a matter of temperamental pessimism versus optimism over human nature. It is mostly a question of the endgame: Why do human beings exist? For what purpose? After all, the notion of nature inescapably indicates purpose. Thus to know what your mind is made for is as significant a question as knowing what you are created for. To know what makes for a good human being tells us what makes for good thoughts. What constitutes "bad" necessarily translates into anything unhelpful for human nature, anything that thwarts our purpose. Although it might not make sense now, throwing out the highest ideal of volitional thought is worth doing here: "One human thought alone is worth more than the entire world, hence God alone is worthy of it."[4] More later on this line from St. John of the Cross. For now, let it gestate in your soul.

In the following chapter we will look at the kind of transformation or renewal of mind called for by the gospel. The Greek New Testament employs the term *metanoia*, normally translated as "repentance," yet its literal meaning refers primarily to a change of mind and heart, of which outward repentance is the sign (see Mk 1:15). Here, we are mainly concerned with identifying the root problem, which we cannot bypass and still "be renewed in the spirit of your minds" (Eph 4:23). St. Teresa of Ávila's thumbnail of it is about as plain as it gets:

> He wants us to love truth; we love the lie. He wants us to desire the eternal; we, here below, lean toward what comes to an end. He wants us to desire sublime and great things; we, here below, desire base and earthly things. He would want us to desire only what is secure; we, here below, love the dubious.[5]

No one is shocked to recognize how commercial advertising exploits all of these leanings. So does the devil, for that matter. And we too easily tilt toward these temporal, doubtful, base things to get us through life. The psychoactive effects of nicotine, for example, are well established: suppression of anxiety, anger, and depression, all within seconds of inhalation.[6] Alcohol has comparable effects. Neither substance is sinful when used in moderation, yet their availability makes them some of the most frequently used (or abused) coping substances. If we were not so distracted and attracted by these quick and easy counterfeits, would the Lord really need to admonish us not to be anxious about food, clothing, aging? Daily and hourly reminders, Lord, are very much appreciated: "Therefore do not be anxious about tomorrow, for tomorrow will be anxious for itself. Let the day's own trouble be sufficient for the day" (Mt 6:34).

Our thought life may be cluttered by these things, but the deeper distrust engendered by our first parents cannot be left unexamined. The Carmelite mystic St. Elizabeth of the Trinity speaks of the need for God's love to consume "all our hostility to Him."[7] That is a stunning word: "hostility." More than resistance it conveys antagonism, even resentment, and opposition. Saints are realists. God, moreover, is not shocked to find hostility in us, any more than he was surprised at Jonah's rage (see Jon 4:8–9). Reflecting honestly on ourselves, by the light of grace, we discern areas in our souls where we harbor bitterness toward the Lord, perhaps owing to missed opportunities, frustrations, loss of advantages that others have received, the defects of our character, inability to do all the things we would like, and so forth. Do we think these will not return and darken our moments of prayer? Can we appreciate how they might prevent us from going deeper in our relationship with God?

Since, as mentioned above, relatively few of us are willing to lay our original disorder at the feet of our first parents, it might be helpful to reiterate here what was apparent to previous generations. Our erratic thought life is at least partially a consequence of our dubious inheritance. As fallen creatures we suffer not only the ultimate penalty of death, but also impaired thinking and willing, faculties intrinsic to prayer. Our human nature, as the *Catechism* puts it, "is wounded in the natural powers proper to it, subject to ignorance, suffering and the dominion of death, and inclined to sin—an inclination to evil that is called concupiscence."[8]

Wound is a helpful word. To have a vulnerability means having a place that is tender to the touch and/or capable of being injured and especially reinjured. Its delicacy requires special care and protection. However much we may wish to be masters of ourselves and our environment, however much we might think willpower alone can immunize us against frailty, we can never entirely banish weakness, the pull of sin, and a lack of clarity in the mind. Healing is required.

Healing for the Christian, however, is not an entirely passive dynamic. We may be weakened, but in another helpful expression, the *Catechism* also insightfully identifies concupiscence as a wrestling partner,[9] and that designation is perfect for the providential function it serves after the Fall. When we struggle against another who is as strong as or stronger than we are, we can either quit because we find the conflict too exacting, or keep at it and become stronger in the process, even if sometimes we are bested. By God's grace, we can even become "more than conquerors through him who loved us" (Rom 8:37). That, in brief, is why God has left us with these handicaps. We only grow through adversity, and the central struggle for each of us is within, against our own disorders and bad inclinations. Opt out of this and you cease to grow "to mature manhood, to the measure of the stature of the fulness of Christ . . . [for] we are to grow up in every way into him who is the head, into Christ" (Eph 4:13, 15).

This is a crucial point. If the foundational cause of the dysfunctional mind is the rebellion of our first parents in the original sin, then the effects will always linger to some degree. Psychology borrows much from evolutionary biology, often to great advantage, but the root problem remains undiscovered by the sciences—while enjoying, to Chesterton's point, overwhelming empirical evidence.

A concluding point from St. Thomas Aquinas solidifies understanding of what manner of control we can exert over our own minds, all things being equal. He helpfully distinguishes between "despotic" and "political" rule over ourselves. Despotic rule is absolute, the way "a man rules his slaves, who have not the right to resist in any way the orders of the one that commands them."[10] Thus, Aquinas says, does the soul rule the body, insofar as those bodily parts which are subject to voluntary movement (such as feet or hands) will move on command and cannot resist the will.

The mind, by contrast, or the power of reason, controls the bodily appetites with a "political" power, characterized by rule over free subjects capable of resisting the reason. Because our appetites are moved by our senses, as well as by the imagination, these powers "do resist reason, inasmuch as we sense or imagine something pleasant, which reason forbids, or unpleasant, which reason commands."[11] Thus even though we are not determined to act according to the disordered inclination, we will likely feel the pull against our reason.

The conflict posed by the rebelliousness of our senses and imagination is a direct result of the loss of original harmony between soul and body in unfallen man. Living in the wake of the Fall, however, it is instructive to know that nothing is particularly wrong with us, over and above original sin, if effort is required to keep our appetites from dictating our actions. The imagination will roam and the appetites will be either attracted by their proper objects or repelled by whatever is disagreeable to them.

St. Teresa won't allow this state of affairs to disturb her peace, even as her interior faculties dart about erratically. She is too humble to be disquieted. Rather, she laughs at herself, nods to the effects of original sin, and keeps loving God amid the chaos.

> At other times I find that I can't even form in a fitting way a thought about God or of any good, or practice prayer, even though I'm in solitude; but I feel that I know him. I understand that it is the intellect and imagination that does me harm here, for the will is all right it seems to me and disposed toward every good. But this intellect is so wild that it doesn't seem to be anything else than a frantic madman no one can tie down nor am I master of it long enough to keep it calm for the space of a Creed. Sometimes I laugh at myself and know my misery, and I look at this madman and leave it alone to see what it does; and—glory to God—it surprisingly enough never turns to evil but to indifferent things: to whether there is anything to do here or there or over yonder.
>
> I often undergo this scattering of the faculties; sometimes I understand clearly that my lack of physical health has much to do with it. I frequently recall the harm original sin did to us; this is the source, I think, of our being incapable of enjoying so much good in an integral way. And my own sins must be a cause; if I hadn't committed so many, I would be more integrated in good.[12]

ENDNOTES

1. G. K. Chesterton, *Orthodoxy* (Dodd, Mead, 1908), p. 7.
2. William R. Miller and Stephen Rollnick, *Motivational Interviewing: Helping People Change*, 3rd ed. (The Guilford Press, 2013), p. 6.

3. Thomas Aquinas, *Summa Theologiae,* trans. Fathers of the English Dominican Province (Benziger, 1947), 1-2.82.2.

4. John of the Cross, *The Sayings of Light and Love*, in *The Collected Works of St. John of the Cross*, p. 88.

5. Teresa of Ávila, *The Way of Perfection*, p. 202.

6. See "Dr. Vincent Felitti: Reflections on the Adverse Childhood Experiences (ACE) Study," posted June 23, 2016, by National Congress of American Indians, YouTube, 32 min., 44 sec., https://www.youtube.com/watch?v=-ns8ko9-ljU.

7. Elizabeth of the Trinity, "Heaven in Faith," in *The Complete Works: Major Spiritual Writings*, vol. 1 (ICS, 1984), p. 96.

8. *Catechism of the Catholic Church*, 2nd ed. (Libreria Editrice Vaticana–United States Conference of Catholic Bishops, 2000), no. 405.

9. *Catechism*, no. 1264.

10. Aquinas, *Summa Theologiae*, 1.81.3-ad2.

11. Aquinas, *Summa Theologiae*, 1.81.3-ad2.

12. Teresa of Ávila, *The Book of Her Life,* p. 261.

FIVE
Cleaning Our Glasses

Flannery O'Connor has another lesson to teach us. In what is probably her best known story, "A Good Man is Hard to Find," she depicts an eminently symbolic action taken by a murderer who has just shot a harmless grandmother three times in the chest. Since O'Connor's stories typically explore the workings of grace in the most distressing, bizarre, and violent circumstances, she shows the killer (called "The Misfit") performing a gesture symbolic of a perspective change, suggestive even of eventual conversion: "Then he put his gun down on the ground and took off his glasses and began to clean them."[1]

Outside of literature, it would be a gesture as ordinary as blowing your nose, and as unworthy of comment. We might class it among the nervous behaviors of one distracting himself from moral reflection, from the distress of a disturbed conscience, and it is certainly that as well. But for our purposes, changing how we think requires cleaning our lenses in more than a symbolic way. How we see or perceive directly influences how we think.

Like The Misfit, it might take a jolt for us to begin critiquing our own thought processes. Patterns of thought typically go uncritiqued until interrupted—until truth or reality break in, to borrow a bit from Robert Frost.[2] In fact, just before The Misfit pulled the trigger, the so-called harmless grandmother also had her moment of change, her metanoia, prompted by the prospect of imminent and violent death. Post mortem, The Misfit comments on the quick transformation he saw, in one of the greatest lines in American literature: "She would of been a good woman, . . . if it had been somebody there to shoot her every minute of her life."[3]

That gun-to-the-head moment forms my introduction to the corrective power of disrupting our pathological thought patterns, with pathological being understood not clinically but broadly as simply unhealthy or distorted ways of thinking. Most of the time our thoughts will not be interrupted and ineluctably focused at gunpoint or before some other crisis situation. Crises come in life, of course, and they do compel us to reassess many aspects of our lives. Most of the time, however, our daily battle with thoughts requires a painstaking effort to critique and test their veracity against the ordinary flow of life.

Whatever we consider stressful, distressing, saddening, desirable, worthy of celebration, and so forth, will continue to be so in our minds until reassessed in the light of new information, new experiences, a greater exposure to the light of truth. This is far from saying that our perceptions are always wrong, but that they are always subject to refinement, even where grosser distortions are not present. Our feelings will follow the meaning-content of our thoughts—that is, what our ideas, beliefs, and perceptions represent about ourselves and the world—and this should give us pause where feelings tend to overpower our reason.

The concept of "reality testing" endorsed by Aaron T. Beck (1921–2021), one of the foremost theoreticians and developers of cognitive behavioral therapy (CBT), involves stepping back or distancing ourselves from our thoughts to evaluate how well they reflect the objective truth of reality against how we perceive it. It is not always clear whether our assessments of events are laser accurate, since human action can be ambiguous and motivation very complicated. Hence the importance of distance and reflection, where time permits, and urgency does not require action. Our prayer time can function as a privileged opportunity to bring our thoughts and feelings before the Lord for reappraisal.

Thomist theologian Benedict Ashley, OP, characterizes the helpfulness of CBT as it pertains to depression, but its application to other negative affective experiences like anxiety is apparent:

> Cognitive therapy has been empirically shown to be the most reliable and effective of methods for treating depression. This makes sense in view of the model of personhood we have described [i.e., the Catholic-Christian model of the human person], since the technique helps a person who has formed various habits or schemas in their use of their memory, imagination, and evaluative senses

> that are excessively negative, and has turned their attention away from more positive imagery. Consequently, the person continually stimulates negative bodily changes and experiences constant negative emotions or feelings. These habits of their stream of consciousness must be replaced by more normal habits.[4]

Replacing unhelpful habits of thought with "more normal" ones is facilitated by creating a reflective distance between our perceptions and thoughts. Spiritual theology teaches that "recollection" (that is, the fostering of interior awareness of God's presence and providence in our lives) can function in this way. Recollection helps us to live in the truth (see 1 Jn 1:6), instead of in darkness and futility of mind (see Rom 1:21; 8:5). An ongoing renewal of mind and heart is envisioned by St. Paul, as he frequently exhorts the first generation of Christians to change the way they think, and highlights as a consequence the actions that issue from distorted or corrupted thinking:

> Put off your old nature which belongs to your former manner of life and is corrupt through deceitful lusts, and be renewed in the spirit of your minds, and put on the new nature, created after the likeness of God in true righteousness and holiness. (Eph 4:22–24)

This connection is recognized no less in psychotherapy, especially as represented by the aforementioned CBT. Beck considers the link between thoughts and emotions as an "essential relation," explaining, "The specific content of the interpretation of an event leads to a specific emotional response."[5] How we interpret events leads to how we feel about them. We all know how two people can perceive the same event or thing in totally divergent ways. A roller coaster is one man's thrill and another man's terror. The interpretive content for the former is of exhilarating but safe fun; the latter interprets the same ride as terrifying and, at least, productive of the *feeling* of danger.

Beck identifies "automatic thoughts" as the unwitting cognitive context inside of which we *unreflectively* interpret our experiences. Whereas our first thoughts may not always be prejudiced by pathological fears or insecurities, our point here is to understand how involuntary but habitual thoughts can disturb our conscious life, and particularly our prayer life. It might never occur to us to question the reflex thoughts we have about ourselves, others, life, God, happiness, and the like. A careful inventory made through recollection is an important step in discerning the good from the bad. It likewise needs to be an ongoing discernment, an attentiveness to our thought motifs.

St. Paul's thorn in the flesh may be a good example here (see 2 Cor 12:7–10). He is compelled to reconceptualize the thorn from a humiliating annoyance to a token or occasion of God's strength. God enlightened his understanding to reevaluate what had been an oppressive limitation (whatever the thorn was) to the mystical umbilical cord connecting the weak child to its source of strength. The thorn remained a thorn, but reimagined in the light of faith, it became an instrument of grace, even an occasion of boasting.

The same is true of the crucifix, the central Christian example of an event or image that means one thing to those without faith and a completely different thing to those enlightened by faith.

> For since, in the wisdom of God, the world did not know God through wisdom, it pleased God through the folly of what we preach to save those who believe. For Jews demand signs and Greeks seek wisdom, but we preach Christ crucified, a stumbling block to Jews and folly to Gentiles, but to those who are called, both Jews and Greeks, Christ the power of God and the wisdom of God. For the foolishness of God is wiser than men, and the weakness of God is stronger than men. (1 Cor 1:21–25)

In the ancient world, Roman crucifixion was the means of inflicting on a criminal the most excruciating, prolonged, and public death possible. It was meant to be seen and feared by the public to deter not only criminal activity but also the insurrection of subject peoples. It was in no way a sacred thing, in no way a spectacle to inspire prayerful meditation. But the power of God is such that he can take the absolutely worst, most unjust event ever perpetrated and transfigure it into the ultimate moment of glory. The script is flipped forever when the Son of Man submits to his passion.

I remember my speechless shock when, as a teenager, a Protestant friend of mine saw the crucifix in my bedroom and vehemently objected, “That’s idolatry. You don’t need things like that.” I had never heard anyone utter the least negative comment about a crucifix. But his religious upbringing had formed him to see all religious images as violations of the second commandment. So that no matter how much the image might piously represent a sacred person or event, using it in the context of worship or prayer, or in any context, was outlawed by divine proscription.

The topic of images here is more than a digression. Catholicism takes images for granted, not as a blatant contradiction of the commandment forbidding depictions of created things in the context of worship, but as an extension of the Incarnation: Christ "is the image of the invisible God" (Col 1:15). Our minds are inevitably populated by images; some people have more, others less, but all have some. We need to replace deceptive, unhelpful images with true ones. One of the reasons why God became man in Christ was precisely to reveal the heavenly Father to us in flesh and blood. Whatever we can do by means of visualizations to keep this fresh and uppermost in our thoughts is very likely a good thing, and need not degenerate into idolatry.[6]

When I subsequently visited the home of this same good friend, I noticed in his room a nicely framed black-and-white poster of Marilyn Monroe. The irony didn't occur to me until years later: *You mean, I'm not allowed to have an image of Jesus crucified to look at, think about, and pray before, but you're allowed to have a photographed image of the twentieth century's most famous sex symbol?* Now, one could object: *Neither is right: neither images of Jesus nor of Marilyn Monroe.* Okay. But surely one is less wrong than the other, no? Even further, couldn't one be positively helpful in our faith life? And does anyone really think that the Incarnation was of benefit only to those who had the privilege of laying eyes on Jesus firsthand, in the first century? For most of Christian history, the answer has been a resounding no. A tour of the Mediterranean world and its ancient Christian churches should resolve the question, at least from a historical point of view.

In no way does Beck, nor do we, imply that the world and our experience of the world lacks any inherent meaning, that meaning attribution is arbitrary. Some modern philosophical currents, and schools of literary criticism, say as much. No, the approach of a ferocious mountain lion when you are hiking alone should inspire extreme fear. The sight of a newborn infant should inspire joy and wonder. These are examples of properly ordered perceptions and their attendant feelings. What we are saying is that any disorder in our perceptions, and our thoughts about them, will lead to emotions that are more or less disordered. Likewise, insofar as our emotional life is dysregulated our perceptions will be obscured by our feelings, creating a vicious circle.

The question of reasonableness and accuracy then becomes a discernment tool: Is there more than one way to understand what I perceive? Would my emotional response be considered reasonable by most people? How do people around me respond to the same things that I see? These are helpful questions, especially if you observe yourself reacting more strongly than others in your environment. Do you, for example, jump at every sudden noise as though it were a threat? Barring a trauma response, which requires special handling, the question is: Is that alarm response appropriate in your particular circumstances, especially if it's going off at the slightest provocation?

If you object that this is precisely the point, that you don't know what is reasonable or appropriate, whether your emotions should express themselves too much or too little, then consulting others is a prudent step toward self-knowledge. Taking counsel need not include specialized care, such as with spiritual direction or consulting a therapist. Ordinarily the people around you should be your first line of self-reflection. Ask your friends and family how they see the things you see, and see what they say.

What is needed, in any case, is an ongoing purification of our spiritual and mental vision:

> The eye is the lamp of the body. So, if your eye is sound, your whole body will be full of light; but if your eye is not sound, your whole body will be full of darkness. If then the light in you is darkness, how great is the darkness! (Mt 6:22–23)

The larger project here is to change the way we think altogether by adopting truer reference points, truer ideals: truth in general, but especially revealed truth, through which lens we see a providence at work that makes us notice the lilies of the field and the birds of the air and innumerable other things. The point is not to lob better thoughts at the bad ones, but to welcome and experience a global transformation wrought by grace.

The renewal of the inner man in Christ, already alluded to previously in Augustine's conversion, is the real scope of ordering our thought life. "The cultivation of good thoughts," writes Fr. Alexis Trader,

> is an essential daily practice that brings order to the motley foliage of the human heart. It aims not at responding to specific thoughts, but at rather refashioning the overall way in which [we] think by turning [our] attention to conceptual categories shaped by revelation.[7]

His brilliantly concise formulation points to the root and branch scope of our overarching goal: "*turning [our] attention to conceptual categories shaped by revelation*." Getting into the habit of referring all things to Divine Providence, to the economy of salvation in Christ, is crucial to the success of our inner transformation. Christian life demands it. We cannot live the life of faith outwardly only, in proximity to holy people and things, but must undergo a full interior regeneration.

Since our minds automatically categorize experiences, categorize our experience of the world around us, those categories need to be the right ones. As Isaiah forcefully puts it: "Woe to those who call evil good and good evil, who put darkness for light and light for darkness, who put bitter for sweet and sweet for bitter" (Is 5:20). To see reality from the higher vantage point of faith enables us to evaluate all things in the truest light of which we are capable:

> The unspiritual man does not receive the gifts of the Spirit of God, for they are folly to him, and he is not able to understand them because they are spiritually discerned. The spiritual man judges all things, but is himself to be judged by no one. "For who has known the mind of the Lord so as to instruct him?" But we have the mind of Christ. (1 Cor 2:14–16)

It is no slight thing to claim to possess "the mind of Christ" as our own. It is given us in baptism, along with all the other graces that make us living images of Jesus. To activate this mentality (if "activate" is the right word) union with Jesus according to his chosen metaphor is key: the vine and the branches (see Jn 15:4–6). In practice, this union comes about through consistent prayer, a desire to know and cooperate with God's will, actively seeking to get beyond saying "Lord, Lord" and into conformity with his providence. This is where progress is found.

I promised in the introduction to return to a quotation from Abbot Nesteros, where he *kind of* promises that after sufficient spiritual progress, "not only every purpose and thought of your heart, but also all the wanderings and rovings of your imagination will become to you a holy and unceasing pondering of the Divine law."[8] Even if one does not reach this rarified state, it is important to underscore the broader truth accessible to us all. Nesteros is not necessarily promising a permanent state of distraction-free prayer (although grace could indeed produce that), but he is providing a framework in which to understand their occurrence.

The apparently random wandering and roving does not fall outside of God's loving watch over us. What does this mean? It means that the order of reality, which is the order of Divine Providence, includes all the cognitive states I endure or enjoy. The rovings of my mind are not divorced from my relationship with God. Like a child exploring the small world of bedroom or backyard, every move is under a parent's watchful eye.

We are seen by God. We are loved as we are seen. "The eyes of the Lord," says Sirach, "are ten thousand times brighter than the sun; they look upon all the ways of men, and perceive even the hidden places. Before the universe was created, it was known to him; so it was also after it was finished" (Sir 23:19–20). Thus our struggle for interior simplicity and purity transpires not in some no-man's-land but under the Lord's merciful gaze.

Anything we do in the spiritual life requires acknowledgement of not so much a divine backdrop before which we act out our life drama, but the deeper metaphysical reality of God as the One in whom "we live and move and have our being" (Acts 17:28). There is no "outside" of God. If we have been baptized into Christ, then what changes is not place but mode of being. We choose to exist in the reality that already encompasses us, but which requires our cooperation for union to take place.

We are in our healer. Our wounds are in some mysterious way discernible in his; for if his wounds heal us, if Jesus took upon himself all our sicknesses, then we need to voluntarily avail ourselves of the healing. As we become aware of how others have hurt us—and what is often more difficult, how we have hurt ourselves—we can begin to experience his healing love from the inside. Healing comes not from the outside, as when we apply treatments or undergo medical procedures. A far more delicate and intimate healing transpires as we wordlessly present ourselves before God and he touches us, deeper than our feelings can report.

An apt comparison may be drawn with the specific type of healing pornography addiction demands. Whereas all addictions possess an emotional component, use of pornography especially signals relational dysfunction: from self-loathing to social withdrawal. Under the brokenness, however, are misdirected and frustrated desires for love and intimacy. Breaking the cycle of promised reward, euphoria, and shame, what the user needs is to feel emotions generated by authentic, human, interpersonal relationships (real emotion, in other words) for a change, flowing from selfless love. He needs real intimacy born of vulnerability, the genuine tenderness that comes from chaste love. We could analyze the experience as a dopaminergic reward response or an artificial hormonal stimulation of oxytocin; it's helpful for an addict to know about these neural, biochemical processes. But in the end, love heals, whether we know the chemical reactions or not. "What," asked Benedict XVI, "could ever save us apart from love?"[9]

St. John Paul II connects interpersonal love with the conformity to Christ called for by the Christian life, specifically how this develops in the prayer of the Rosary. Empathy with Christ and the Blessed Mother is fostered. If empathy is typically understood as the effort to feel the feelings of another by entering their experience without immediate commentary or judgment, then meditation on the mysteries of the Rosary has the potential to transform how we think and feel in the deepest possible levels of human experience.

> Christian spirituality is distinguished by the disciple's commitment to become conformed ever more fully to his Master. . . . a growing assimilation which will increasingly shape the conduct of the disciple in accordance with the "mind" of Christ: "Have this mind among yourselves, which was in Christ Jesus" (Phil 2:5). In the words of the

> Apostle, we are called "to put on the Lord Jesus Christ" (Rom 13:14; Gal 3:27).
>
> In the spiritual journey of the Rosary, based on the constant contemplation—in Mary's company—of the face of Christ, this demanding ideal of being conformed to him is pursued through an association which could be described in terms of friendship. We are thereby enabled to enter naturally into Christ's life and as it were to share his deepest feelings.[10]

We mentioned earlier how we can regard good or bad thoughts as supporting the goals of our nature or thwarting them. In conclusion to this chapter, a last point on strategy follows from mention of the Rosary, which Pope Leo XIII compared to "a most powerful warlike weapon"[11] in the late nineteenth century. Counter measures may be preemptive or launched in the midst of a conflict. Having an arsenal of counter thoughts when unhelpful or tempting ones disturb us is of ancient tradition, as witnessed particularly by Evagrius of Pontus in his handbook of scriptural verses for use in spiritual warfare.[12] It is a treasury of biblical counter-thoughts directed against the eight faults or vices mentioned above, under the heading of *the thoughts*. Such an alignment shows how closely the Church Fathers considered our thought life as bearing upon our feelings and actions.

Unlike old and familiar strategies that an adversary might sniff out and repel, the use of Scripture always retains its power against the evil spirits. Jesus fended off the devil's temptations in the desert by citing Scripture, modeling spiritual combat for us. Biblical texts possess an effective sacramental quality that the deceptions of the evil one can never outwit or overpower, because the words are those of God, spirit-breathed, potent, and alive: "For the word of God is living and active, sharper than any two-edged sword" (Heb 4:12).

Although Evagrius does the lion's share of work for us, the most potent strategy is to search the Scriptures yourself to identify the verses to which the Holy Spirit draws your attention. Evagrius, among other Fathers, would tell you nothing different. Seek and you will find.

ENDNOTES

1. Flannery O'Connor, "A Good Man is Hard to Find" in *The Complete Stories*, p. 132.

2. See Robert Frost, "Birches," Poetry Foundation, accessed at https://www.poetryfoundation.org/poems/44260/birches.

3. O'Connor, "A Good Man is Hard to Find," p. 133.

4. Benedict M. Ashley, *Healing for Freedom: A Christian Perspective on Personhood and Psychotherapy* (The Institute for the Psychological Sciences Press, 2013), p. 322.

5. Aaron T. Beck, *Cognitive Therapy and the Emotional Disorders* (Meridian/Penguin, 1979), p. 51.

6. Aquinas, *Summa Theologiae*, 3.25.3.

7. Alexis Trader, *Ancient Christian Wisdom and Aaron Beck's Cognitive Therapy: A Meeting of Minds* (Peter Lang, 2012), p. 220. Fr. Trader's book is a masterful and sophisticated exposition of the intersection between ancient patristic thought and Beck's therapeutic model.

8. Cassian, The First Conference of Abbot Nesteros, p. 442.

9. Benedict XVI, Address on the Occasion of the XX World Youth Day: Youth Vigil in Cologne (August 18, 2005). https://www.vatican.va.

10. John Paul II, Apostolic Letter to to the Bishops, Clergy, and Faithful on the Most Holy Rosary *Rosarium Virginis Mariae* (October 16, 2002), no. 15. https://www.vatican.va.

11. Leo XIII, Encyclical on Devotion to the Rosary *Supremi Apostolatus Officio* (September 1, 1883), no. 3. https://www.vatican.va.

12. Evagrius of Pontus, *Talking Back* (*Antirrhêtikos*): *A Monastic Handbook for Combating Demons*, trans. David Brakke (Liturgical Press, 2009). Also referenced in my book, *Praying from the Depths of the Psalms* (Scepter, 2019).

SIX
Répondez s'il vous plaît

Now we have received not the spirit of the world,
but the Spirit which is from God, that we might
understand the gifts bestowed on us by God.
—1 Corinthians 2:12

And on receiving it they
grumbled at the householder.
—Matthew 20:11

The unspiritual man does not receive
the gifts of the Spirit of God.
—1 Corinthians 2:14

If "God loves a cheerful giver" (2 Cor 9:7), he also loves a grateful receiver. The Samaritan leper who returned to give thanks to Jesus for his healing was praised as much for his gratitude as for his faith (Lk 17:11–19). In St. Peter's language, grateful reception is a matter of being "good stewards of God's varied grace" (1 Pt 4:10). Knowing how to receive a gift is a social grace we learn as children. Saying thank you, writing thank you cards, are ways we learn to express gratitude to a benefactor.

This chapter is not exactly on gratitude, but on its inseparable companion in the spiritual life: receptivity. One cannot be grateful without first being aware of having received. St. Paul is emphatic about this: "What have you that you did not receive? If then you received it, why do you boast as if it were not a gift" (1 Cor 4:7)? Countless are the times the New Testament speaks of gifts given and received, yet the latter posture is not always punctuated with the receptivity that bears fruit.

Receptivity, in spiritual language, is not only a necessary disposition for prayer but is also needful when addressing our thoughts constructively. If we are closed off to the Lord in any way, then our thoughts will be locked into a sterile microenvironment into which the life-giving Word of God cannot enter and change us. To be deliberately closed off means that we find certain thoughts unacceptable, literally unthinkable, so that we remain stuck in a self-defeating circuit, in tight cognitive patterns shielded from enlightenment.

An illustration of the "unacceptable" in the present context comes from a very wise priest I know, a spiritual director as well as a clinical psychologist, who sometimes initiates a session with a directee with one or other of these questions: "What would you least like to talk about today?" Or, "What would you least like God to ask of you?" What emerges from that is the raw material of our response to God, the unfiltered contents of our interior life set against the will we fear to follow, the direction we would rather avoid taking. The quality and depth of our receptivity are brought into high relief when encountering what it was made for: the will of God.

Sometimes this situation occurs because an individual thinks he is well formed in the faith but in reality has some deficits in knowledge. Whenever we experience our ignorance about something, insecurity is a natural consequence, and some find that insecurity intolerable. We are not referring so much to unchangeable dogmatic truths as to a frame of mind threatened by the prophetic force of God's Word and the changes that Word will require of us. It would be very appropriate to begin our time of prayer with an explicit declaration of openness to the Lord: *My mind and my heart are open to You, O Lord*, or "Speak, LORD, for thy servant hears" (1 Sm 3:9).

If we pray in the Psalms that God will open our eyes to see the wonders of his law, and if Jesus himself needed to open the minds of the Emmaus disciples to understand the Scriptures, then we can insert ourselves into this somewhat vulnerable position to receive the light and direction God wishes to give us. You cannot escape the need for intentional receptivity since our hearts harden and our minds grow dull if left to themselves. This is one reason why every hour of the Liturgy of the Hours begins with a cry for God's speedy assistance. Practitioners of the Office will tell you that attention and devotion are neither assumed nor automatic. What St. Benedict called the "opus Dei" (the *work of God*) is truly work, demanding focus and effort.

To read a book such as this, or any book designed to facilitate meditation on sacred truths, is already to declare our openness to the Lord—and even more to the point, to make big strides in the reconquest of our minds for Christ. You are already doing the very thing for which you picked up this book. As St. Teresa of Ávila says about reading and mental prayer: "Reading is very helpful for recollection and serves as a necessary substitute—even though little may be read—for anyone who is unable to practice mental prayer."[1] She frankly acknowledges that some people need to depend on a text rather than engage in parrying distracting thoughts for the space of their prayer time. As long as the text is directing our minds and hearts to God, its use can be far more fecund than sitting with eyes closed while the imagination throws up the wreckage of memories and unresolved conflicts.

That is why these pages are more than a kind of instruction manual for eliminating the unwelcome between our ears. Everything we say here is couched in the context of Scripture, spiritual theology, sound psychology, and especially Divine Providence. What we do with our minds is not divorced or isolated from our relationship with God or our general spiritual and psychological health.

Openness can take physical and liturgical forms. Have you ever seen someone at prayer with arms extended and palms opened upward? From a liturgical standpoint, Eastern Christians typically pray in this posture, whether they are clergy or laity. Years ago an Armenian bishop corrected my posture at the altar during the divine liturgy, as I was learning to celebrate it in his cathedral. I had extended my hands after the manner of Latin-rite priests, more or less upright and stiff at the breast. He said that the Latin posture accentuates offering, whereas the Eastern stance manifests receptivity. Neither excludes the other, of course, but the ancient cultures out of which each liturgy emerged emphasize one mode of prayer over the other.

Private prayer, too, demands such a posture, at least in spirit. A radical receptivity to God transforms the way we think (or even if we think discursively at all) during prayer. If it feels like distracting thoughts are things that get in the way while we're trying to do this activity called prayer, the mode of reception reverses the direction and makes us see the true origin of prayer. Our activity is very much secondary as we receive the life-giving sap that flows from the true vine to its rather spindly offshoots (see Jn 15:5).

We should approach prayer with intentionality and appropriate effort, but always with detachment, that it may be what God wants it to be, not necessarily what will satisfy my sense of accomplishment. Most of us expect our prayer to afford us the conviction that we have communicated with God, that he has spoken and we have listened. But prayer takes place on a far deeper level than we can sense, just as communication can transpire on unspoken levels between two people who know each other intimately. God communicates to us without needing words, images, and sensations to get himself across. As we mature spiritually we develop the ability to perceive this profound communication on deeper levels than those we normally use for the day's ordinary interpersonal exchanges.

God can get very small. God can make himself completely invisible and imperceptible to us. The needle's eye is far too spacious for his passage. He makes no noise but that of the barely perceptible breeze, so gentle that a smoldering flame keeps burning in his presence.

Our detachment from communicating on levels of word and image helps us resist the frustration that often accompanies the words, images, and thoughts we don't want. We can let them go without fearing that our prayer has been detoured by them. We can let them come, too, insofar as we humbly recognize that the entrances into our imagination cannot keep out everything undesirable. But between the coming and going, our calm choice can and should always be to show the undesirables the door.

Inevitably, as prayer life develops, we transition from lots of activity and busyness to stillness and passivity—not lethargy and carelessness, but an active receptivity to God's movements in the soul. What continues to grow in us is the flame of love in the heart, even when our feelings seem cold and dead. This is why Christian prayer does not seek inner stillness for its own sake, much less a vacuity of mind, but rather detachment from distracting affections and interests, so that pure love can grow into the gospel flame the Lord so desires to see consuming the whole earth (see Lk 12:49). He touches off the flame, but it is the heart's combustible material that spreads it. "'*Et in meditatione mea exardescit ignis.*'—'And in my meditation a fire shall flame out.' That is why you go to pray: to become a bonfire, a living flame giving heat and light."[2]

For us who are seeking progress in prayer, we know that the dynamic of receptivity requires an increasing willingness to accept God's will. When we pray, we know that we are not engaging in a pious hobby but involving ourselves in the deepest possible transformation: asking for the grace to see ourselves and our circumstances in the light of God's will and for the courage and prudence to make the changes we need to make. This exacting work is never completely over and done with. I sometimes get mildly suspicious when people tell me, excitedly, how much they love to pray. I think, perhaps too skeptically, that they've not yet felt the Lord "meddling" in their lives through both the inspirations and challenges with which he confronts the soul in prayer. An old joke highlights the difference between prayer that we enjoy and prayer that exacts a price. A congregant made uncomfortable by a preacher's message complained to a neighbor: "At a certain point the preacher stopped preaching and started meddling!"

God is not limited in his power and willingness to give, but we limit our capacity to receive by a stingy unwillingness to be transformed by his goodness and generosity, almost as though we don't believe he could be so good to us. St. John of the Cross speaks of the soul's diminished capacity for God owing to disordered attachments to created things.[3] Just as two contraries cannot coexist in the same person, as in loving God with the totality of your heart and something else with the same totality (without the necessary subordination that hierarchy imposes), so our capacity for God is limited by affections that fall outside of him.

Here, Jordan Peterson's sophisticated intuition on the nature of petitionary prayer really clarifies the problem. A precondition exists, if you would pray effectively: You must renounce all that is incompatible with your request. On the verse "Ask, seek, knock," Peterson challenges us to question the quality of our prayer: Do we want to receive gifts without also wanting to change ourselves in the process? Does God ever give gifts without an at least implicit invitation to change?

About "Ask, seek, knock" he comments:

> This is not a casual statement. It is not naive. It is not a matter of asking for a present, unearned. God is no granter of casual wishes. It is a matter, first, of truly Asking. This means being willing to let go of anything and everything that is not in keeping with the desire. Otherwise there is no Asking. There is only an immature and too-often resentful whim and wish: "Oh, that I could have what I want, without doing what is necessary." That will not suffice. So, to ask, seek, and knock is to do everything required to gather what has been left unfinished and to complete it, now. And to ask, seek, and knock is, as well, to determine what must be asked for. And that has to be something that is worthy of God. Why else would it be granted? How else could it possibly be granted?[4]

A prayer worthy of God is one that changes the one praying into a receiver: not a taker or collector, not a mercenary, not one who grabs and goes, but a soul capable of receiving graciously what God gives. Graciously means more than *politely.* When receiving from a benefactor, the recipient is normally obliged to use the gift according to the intention of the donor. In nonprofit organizations, this is a golden rule. In prayer, this inevitably requires us to keep a loose grip on our expectations, preferences, and judgments. It demands of us the disposition of a disciple, which is one of humble surrender and service. It counteracts all of the tendencies we have toward self-assertion and self-preoccupation, all that goes into making ourselves the center of the world.

> When he had washed their feet, and taken his garments, and resumed his place, he said to them, "Do you know what I have done to you? You call me Teacher and Lord; and you are right, for so I am. If I then, your Lord and Teacher, have washed your feet, you also ought to wash one another's feet. For I have given you an example, that you also should do as I have done to you. Truly, truly, I say to you, a servant is not greater than his master; nor is he who is sent greater than he who sent him. If you know these things, blessed are you if you do them. (Jn 13:12–17)

It is crucial to understand that prayer gravitationally pulls us toward the model of Christ as Servant. If we think progress in the spiritual life will land us at some other destination, we will be continually puzzled as to why all our paths keep leading us back onto this narrow road. You are not lost in a labyrinth if you continue to find yourself returning to the lowest place and finding that Christ has already beat you there and is already at work. Prayer attunes us to the myriad opportunities for surrender and service in the humblest of daily circumstances.

For many people prayer is simply asking for what we cannot obtain on our own. We are in need—of health, finances, love, a new home or car—and so we turn to the One who has the power to give what we cannot get for ourselves. This is one dimension of prayer, and it is obviously not our main focus here.

It is a gateway to a relationship with God, probably the most common way by which people find their way into a church, a monastery, and end up on their knees in need. It might be the last resort. But God will take us at whatever point we perceive our need for him. No question.

However, he will not let us walk away thinking that that's all there is to him: power and gift-giving. The relationship with God delineated by Jesus in the Gospels is preeminently one of Father to son, Father to child. In the same breath that he tells us to ask, he also tells us not to worry about materialities, but instead to cultivate a relationship of trusting dependence upon the Father. It is in this sense that Peterson's comment may apply in a unique way: We are not only called to grow by making meaningful changes in our lives to accommodate God's will (as in, whatever we are praying for), but even more importantly, to cultivate the disposition of a child toward the Father.

Receiving Versus Consuming

What frequently thwarts our receptivity in the contemporary world is the mile-wide, inch-deep character of the world wide web, at least in its most popular forms.

Why is it that prayer sometimes looks like a busy internet news page rather than what some Church Fathers call a deep, limpid ocean, calm to the depths, teeming with an ordered movement of life? Since the vast majority of people get their information, news, and entertainment from online sources, the question could be put in terms of inner stillness, which overuse of networks such as the internet destabilizes. In this case there is no mystery. We have trained our memories and imaginations to operate just like what we stare at for hours on end. Either glow like Moses before the tabernacle or reflect the backlighting of the computer screen; the choice remains ours.

Much is made in the literature of the spiritual life on the contrast between the pace and superficiality of modern life vis-à-vis the interior life of prayer, which is not measured by speed, except by the "pace of the Holy Spirit," to paraphrase St. Bernard of Clairvaux. The idea is that we, especially in the West, have so adopted a lifestyle dependent on devices like cell phones, laptops, and other high-speed technologies that the way we think and feel about what makes life enjoyable or even livable has derailed our ability to pray. The expectation of everything on demand is a tyranny under which prayer life cannot survive, let alone flourish.

This is true, to an extent. We intuitively understand that whatever we call prayer requires some measure of focus, devotion, stillness, and quiet. The technologies mentioned above by no means foster these elements and even militate against them. The problem this engenders is crucial to understand for the development of the spiritual life: We can never get deep enough to pray beyond saying words if our minds are frequently elsewhere, our emotions running and jumping all over the map. The technologies, useful as they are, captivate the imagination, diminish impulse control, and thus hijack the very faculties we need to get behind the words we say in prayer.

To some extent these tendencies are present in every generation. Fascination with the immediate and ephemeral is not a novel phenomenon and was not unknown in New Testament times. This description of first-century Athens could fit any number of peoples and places at any point in history: "Now all the Athenians and the foreigners who lived there spent their time in nothing except telling or hearing something new" (Acts 17:21). This introduces the setting in which St. Paul delivers his brief but famous discourse regarding the unknown god, a discourse received by only a few out of the crowd gathered at the Areopagus that day.

We lose the ability to be receptive, even as we are consumers. Mere use of a given object, a present, does not indicate we have received with the depth necessary for true receptivity. To receive, in the spiritual life, is to be changed by the gift. It is not simply to enjoy a favor, because everything given by God to us is a grace, and grace is given not to be neglected, admired, or studied, but to transform the receiver.

As we conclude, a possible objection might surface here. Does not Jesus himself tell us to ask so as to receive—indeed to "ask anything" in his name (Jn 14:14; 16:23; 1 Jn 5:14)? It sounds like he wants us to be quick about our requests to receive, in turn, quick answers. Combined with a teaching on the efficacy of prayer is a promise to deliver.

But to pray in the name of Jesus means to seek his mind and heart. You cannot separate his identity—his "name"—from his thinking and willing, knowing and loving. The conditions for prayer are: "If you abide in me, and my words abide in you, ask whatever you will, and it shall be done for you" (Jn 15:7). This takes prayer to a deeper level than only asking for things. God is indeed free and generous in his gifts; we should absolutely pray whether we consider ourselves deeply spiritual or not. We should not be ignorant, however, of the Lord's endgame: He wants us to be united to him in love. The favors we ask for are just a means to that end.

ENDNOTES

1. Teresa of Ávila, *The Book of Her Life*, p. 68.

2. Josemaría Escrivá, *The Way*, in *The Way, Furrow, The Forge* (Scepter, 2011), no. 92.

3. John of the Cross, *The Ascent of Mount Carmel*, in *The Collected Works of St. John of the Cross*, p. 130.

4. Jordan B. Peterson, *Beyond Order: 12 More Rules for Life* (Penguin Random House UK, 2021), p. 261. Edward Leen likewise echoes our point here: "[Prayer] implies a readiness on our part to abandon what in us is incompatible with what is bestowed by God." *The Vine and the Branches* (Cluny Media, 2025), p. 95.

SEVEN
Of Mind and Monastery: Guarding the Senses

After considering the inward disposition of receptivity, the *sine qua non* of prayer, this chapter will look outward to the environments in which we live and pray. Hence, we will explore the most receptive of all settings: the monastic.

This is more than the author's bias at work. Monasteries are structured to be settings par excellence for the soul's encounter with God. Monasteries are designed to foster silence, solitude, and prayer, absent many of the ordinary distractions found in the world. These qualities all happily conspire to turn the soul toward God, which is why visitors to monasteries normally experience a mixture of peace and agitation. Peace, because of the setting. Agitation, because in the absence of common distractions, one must face the Lord without much external interruption. Be careful what you wish for: Many who want peace and quiet find the ambient surprisingly disconcerting. Clearly, a void opens and where the normal fillers are lacking, the mind and heart untrained in the ways of prayer may not recognize absence as presence where God is concerned.

Identifying the ideal setting is not the same as asserting the ideal response of all who live in it. Effort, intentionality, and striving are always demanded of us. Holiness does not just happen any more than prayer just happens. A mind and heart need to say yes to God in an ongoing way for both prayer and holiness to become habits and, finally, states of being. The holy man, the man of prayer, is a saint, which is the ideal destiny of everyone.

But the place does not automatically produce all of the good things it was built for. Sooner or later those who live in ideal settings recognize that neither peace nor joy nor happiness nor holiness penetrate the soul the way sunlight passes through a window. The goods we seek must be desired, pursued, and welcomed only and exactly in the ways in which God wishes to give them.

Our receptivity can be helped or hindered by the settings we choose for prayer. I emphasize the volitional aspect because seldom can we adapt the environment to ourselves to any kind of perfection. The circumstances in which we live and pray will always be relatively good or bad for the same reason that our minds don't work so well: the fallen world thing.

Our thoughts, whatever their quality, take some of their character from our environment. I have always found Dr. Murray Bowen's astute observation about family culture helpful in assessing the emotional health of any community environment:

All family members live under the same "emotional skin."[1] The (especially) strong emotional output of one member affects the whole, sometimes imperceptibly, but truly. Stress, for example, can be generated by one person's volatility without others being entirely aware of the extent to which it affects them. One may not fully appreciate the extent of the influence until removed from the tense environment into a more relaxed setting.

It follows that our understanding of what's wrong on the inside risks incompleteness if we have little appreciation of how to grapple with our circumstances: cultural, familial, personal, and the like. Ploughing and reseeding our souls will do us little good if we are unaware that an enemy is sowing weeds whenever we're not looking. Even worse, that we are making it easy for him to come and go, lacing our inner life with unhelpful thoughts born of environmental factors. Circumspection, keeping our eyes open and heart vigilant, is key.

This is where the monastery comes into view.

Since popular cultural is tyrannically noisy and commercial, and the protection of our senses becomes a full-time job, some insight may be gained from the monastic context, in which a tiny fraction of the world's population lives. Looking to what people do who remove themselves from the trends of popular culture to live a life focused on God and the spiritual life can help the majority who do not live in monasteries adapt their spiritual lives according to these standards of religious practice.

It is well to note that over the last half-century Church documents have increasingly invoked the need for the cultivation of silence as a precondition for finding God. The commotion of modern life is frequently seen, not exactly as demonic, but as certainly a useful tool for the powers of darkness. Loudness is not really the problem so much as stimulating and provocative forms of entertainment that effectively hyperstimulate the craving for ever more stimulation, with ever diminishing returns.

Since most people outside the circles of consecrated persons are unlikely to know of this older document from Pope St. Paul VI on the renewal of the religious life, I provide an extended excerpt relevant to all who pray:

> . . . Many people, including many of the young, have lost sight of the meaning of their lives and are anxiously searching for the contemplative dimension of their being. They do not realize that Christ, through His Church, can respond to their expectations. Facts of this kind should cause you to reflect seriously on what men have the right to expect of you—you who have formally committed yourselves to a life in the service of the Word, "the true light that enlightens all men." Be conscious then of the importance of prayer in your lives and learn to devote yourselves to it generously. Faithfulness to daily prayer always remains for each one of you a basic necessity. It must have a primary place in your constitutions and in your lives.
>
> The interior man is aware that times of silence are demanded by love of God. As a rule he needs a certain solitude so that he may hear God "speaking to his heart." It must be stressed that a silence which is a mere absence of noise and words, in which the soul cannot renew its

> vigor, would obviously lack any spiritual value. It could even be harmful to fraternal charity, if at that moment it were essential to have contact with others. On the contrary, the search for intimacy with God involves the truly vital need of a silence embracing the whole being, both for those who must find God in the midst of noise and confusion and for contemplatives. Faith, hope and a love for God which is open to the gifts of the Spirit, and also a brotherly love which is open to the mystery of others, carry with them an imperative need for silence.[2]

Silence needs to be learned, as does knowing how to find meaning within the silence and solitude of monastic life. This is equivalent to saying "finding God" in an environment whose sole purpose is that discovery. Lose the sense of God and you lose the one meaning to which all lesser meanings adhere. Lose the sense of God and life fragments into random interests and hobbies, plunging into things I like and enduring things I dislike, without any particular goal in view. Apart from the short term goal of just making it through the day with minimal suffering, how could there be?

The life project of a monastic religious is more than a project: It is a vocation in the most exact sense of the term. It is not *a* calling, but *the* calling. The summons of God is ultimately the only call worthy of the name, since all of the most important calls are his to make: He calls all creation into existence, calls all the living to himself, and one day will call all of us from the grave.

The dynamics of call-and-response within religious life are comprehensive. We not only come to know God in responding but ourselves as respondents. As soon as the Lord begins beckoning us from here to there, to do this or that, we sense whether we are up to the task or not: We experience fear, trembling, and anxiety, or alternatively joy and enthusiasm. We come to know not only the God who calls but the man or woman whose name he knows, whose identity and capabilities are plain to him. We learn that we cannot respond in any adequate way without self-knowledge, and it is (perhaps paradoxically) the call itself that manifests us to ourselves more than anything else.

If the day's schedule includes fixed hours of prayer, my liberty of spirit or selfishness is made clear by my response. Whatever else is chosen for me throughout the day is another occasion of self-observation: I see what the obligation brings out of me and I am made to ponder my identity as a putative servant of God. We can serve ourselves in the religious life instead of higher ideals, and this is a frightening fact. Self-knowledge, clearly, is not always good news. Finding what we are capable of can be downright distressing and immobilizing. But the purpose of that knowledge, in God's eyes, is not that we cower in the dust but let him raise us up.

The foregoing reveals how the challenge to settle down and quiet oneself so as to respond better to the Lord is not absent but brought into high relief in the monastery. This is especially so among novice religious who are making the difficult transition from the variety and vanity of the world to the sameness of the cloister. Those entering the seminary or religious life over the last few decades come from the high-speed, digital world, and their path to interior order is no less fraught with difficulty than the person in the world who simply wants to pray the Rosary or make an hour of Adoration without spending the whole time thinking about something other than Jesus and Mary. How do candidates for religious life manage?

A good portion of formation in a religious house, a monastery or convent, is devoted to quieting down the inner man (see Eph 3:16). The first steps of this process are environmental. The house itself fosters silence in corridors and common places; lengthy times of prayer are required; sources of distraction, especially those of the media, are either strictly curtailed or removed altogether. What's left are you and your thoughts. For many this can initially be an intolerable situation. There are simply too many gaps, silences, spaces, with nothing to fill them, except the nervous energy that attends adjustment from regular sense stimulation to the deliberate calming of the senses, appetites, and emotions. That's a verbose way of saying *withdrawal.*

Silence needs to be learned. Many do not know how or why to seek it, or what to do with it once your immediate environment is, in fact, quiet. External silence is only the first step. Inner silence is the goal. The analogy is plain: Stillness and quiet on the outside should reflect the same qualities on the inside. But as long as thoughts and desires take control, are restless, to that extent inner silence will be thwarted.

We learn through our senses, and our senses (remember original sin?) want gratification all the time, often in disordered ways. Giving them free reign is dangerous if we want to live not only a refined spiritual life but also a more sensitive intellectual and emotional life. In the end the mutual influence helps bring about integration of emotions, thoughts, faculties, and actions—or their misuse can accelerate the fragmentation of the self, largely controlled by whatever our dominant emotion happens to be at the time.

St. Josemaría was not writing to monks but to Christians immersed in the world when he advised: "Silence is the doorkeeper of the interior life."[3] To a spiritual son of his he wrote:

> "My affairs buzz around in my head at the most inopportune moments," you say. That is why I have recommended you to try to establish some times for interior silence . . . and to guard your external and internal senses.[4]

In the monastery these are the first stages of growth, accompanied by the pains of purification and renunciation. This is not the same as white-knuckling, which has more to do with external self-control, hanging on or enduring, instead of interior growth. Once you have some clarity about what is vain versus what really matters, you affectively renounce the former by refusing to indulge the memories or sensations associated with them. Some white-knuckling might be a part of that, of course, but only temporarily until virtues are formed and the tranquility of order begins to overtake the soul. I've made it sound easy, but it is often like peeling away skin: slow, painful, excruciating.

We slowly learn that all the distractions we once depended on in the world to keep us entertained and at least marginally happy were really empty and ephemeral. Admittedly, it is difficult for people to see this with any decent clarity until they remove themselves or retreat from it and, at the same time, taste the good things of God. By comparison, all other things lose their savor:

> I count everything as loss because of the surpassing worth of knowing Christ Jesus my Lord. For his sake I have suffered the loss of all things, and count them as refuse, in order that I may gain Christ and be found in him. (Phil 3:8–9)

No, not all media or popular forms of entertainment are evil. But they are also not particularly helpful in forming Christ within us (see Gal 4:19). In fact, their too frequent use can be detrimental. As the body responds to diet so does the soul to external stimuli: What we absorb through the senses shapes how we think, feel, speak, and act.

Thomas Merton, writing about the relatively new technology called "TV" in 1962, opined:

> Certainly, it would seem that TV could become a kind of unnatural surrogate for contemplation: a completely inert subjection to vulgar images, a descent to a subnatural passivity rather than an ascent to a supremely active passivity in understanding and love. It would seem that television should be used with extreme care and discrimination by anyone who might hope to take interior life seriously.[5]

What might he have to say about Internet and social media?

When I first started writing this book, I thought that, to some, the relevance of the topic may seem questionable if not downright shortsighted: to treat of a topic only pious people encounter during their devotions when "the world," in St

Teresa of Ávila's words, "is all in flames."[6] Let it be said that she herself didn't think it inappropriate to do the very same thing amid the religious and political tumult of the sixteenth century: to write books on prayer and spiritual perfection for her fellow cloistered Carmelite nuns. If the world in some mysterious but real way depends on the prayers of the relative few, then perhaps the quality of those prayers is worth improving.

I can say from the experience of living in a monastery for many years that legions of people do in fact depend on us for prayerful intercession at absolutely the worst and most trying moments of their lives. They ask with confidence, if not some desperation, and they deserve prayers equally serious: less like a hectic internet page and more like Christ's in the garden of his agony. The Church believes that her public prayer, the sacred liturgy, and the private prayers of countless faithful effectively intercede for the salvation of the world. We are in the realm of faith here, granted, but not of make-believe. Many lives have been changed by prayer, and these changes are not the product of wishful thinking.

As a further support for this endeavor, St. Teresa's contemporary and good friend St. John of the Cross might also be enlisted in a quote we have already encountered: "One human thought alone is worth more than the entire world, hence God alone is worthy of it."[7] If this does not exactly reflect how you and I habitually use our thoughts, it at least sets the bar as high as it can be set and gives us an ideal to strive for. It likewise echoes St Paul's admonition, no less absolute: "Set your minds on things that are above, not on things that are on earth" (Col 3:2), and "whatever is true, whatever is honorable, whatever is just, whatever is pure, whatever is lovely, whatever is gracious, if there is any excellence, if there is anything worthy of praise, think about these things" (Phil 4:8).

The monastic life is a setup. We are made to sink or swim according to St. Teresa's uncompromising claim that *God alone suffices*: "Dios solo basta."[8] Where he does not suffice for me, where I do not allow him to, I cannot get by *not* thinking about the cognitive dissonance at work, to borrow the language of psychology. All aspects of monastic life force the soul's relationship with God into the open, where hiding is not an option since there's no place left: "Whither shall I go from thy Spirit? Or whither shall I flee from thy presence" (Ps 139:7)? We have come here not to hide but to live exposed to the truth, to live in God. All prayer should make us stand so vulnerably before the Lord that we can finally give our honest selves to him and receive him fully into ourselves, into selves no longer obscured by masks, deceptions, or noise, but stripped of their defenses and ready to surrender.

ENDNOTES

1. "Introduction to the Eight Concepts," The Bowen Center for the Study of the Family, accessed March 17, 2026, https://www.thebowencenter.org/introduction-eight-concepts.

2. Paul VI, Apostolic Exhortation on the Renewal of the Religious Life according to the Teaching of the Second Vatican Council *Evangelica Testificatio* (June 29, 1971), nos. 45–46. https://www.vatican.va.

3. Escrivá, *The Way*, no. 281.

4. Josemaría Escrivá, *Furrow* (Scepter, 2002), no. 670.

5. Thomas Merton, *New Seeds of Contemplation* (New Directions, 1962), p. 86.

6. Teresa of Ávila, *The Way of Perfection*, p. 43.

7. John of the Cross, *The Sayings of Light and Love*, no. 35.

8. Teresa of Ávila, "Nada te turbe," in *The Collected Works of St. Teresa of Ávila*, vol. 3, trans. Kieran Kavanaugh and Otilio Rodriguez (ICS, 1985), p. 386.

EIGHT

Love and War: Distractions

Now these are the nations which the LORD left,
to test Israel by them, that is, all in Israel who
had no experience of any war in Canaan; it was
only that the generations of the people of Israel
might know war, that he might teach war to
such at least as had not known it before.
—Judges 3:1–2

From surrender to teaching and knowing war? Long-standing Catholic social doctrine acknowledges such a thing as just war, and certain qualifications must be met before one nation may engage another belligerent or hostile state in battle. In the spiritual life war is waged as a rule of conduct. There is no trouble-free or war-free spiritual zone, nor is there much of a no-man's-land: The battle follows us more or less wherever we go. St. Paul encourages St. Timothy to "wage the good warfare" (1 Tm 1:18), and Sirach admonishes a youth: "My son, if you come forward to serve the Lord, prepare yourself for temptation" (2:1).

In translation, this is not equivalent to saying that our cortisol levels should be continually elevated, nor muscles permanently tensed. Rather it alerts us to the fact that attempting to avoid all conflict is a recipe for insanity in any domain of life. Highly agreeable people tend to recoil from conflict because of the threat it poses to their security. To accept conflict, conversely, means accepting an inevitable amount of insecurity in life—even to invite it—and this is simply to come to terms with reality: Life is uncertain, precarious, and subject to innumerable variables, both positive and negative. To avoid conflict altogether also means refusing to grow, possibly refusing to grow up at all.

Learning to be battle ready is God's will for us, as the passage from Judges indicates. But it means arming ourselves with strength and strategy that relies on the Lord, whatever the present moment might entail.

> Blessed be the LORD, my rock,
> who trains my hands for war,
>   and my fingers for battle;
> my rock and my fortress,
>   my stronghold and my deliverer,
> my shield and he in whom I take refuge,
>   who subdues the peoples under him. (Ps 144:1–2)

This pairs well with St. Paul's famous exhortation to faith, prayer, and vigilance as symbolized in a warrior's armor:

> . . . be strong in the Lord and in the strength of his might. Put on the whole armor of God, that you may be able to stand against the wiles of the devil. For we are not contending against flesh and blood, but against the principalities, against the powers, against the world rulers of this present darkness, against the spiritual hosts of wickedness in the heavenly places. Therefore take the whole armor of God, that you may be able to withstand in the evil day, and having done all, to stand. Stand therefore, having girded your loins with truth, and having put on the breastplate of righteousness, and having shod your feet with the equipment of the gospel of peace; above all taking the shield of faith, with which you can quench all the flaming darts of the evil one. And take the helmet of salvation, and the sword of the Spirit, which is the word of God. Pray at all times in the Spirit, with all prayer and supplication. To that end keep alert with all perseverance. . . . (Eph 6:10–18)

We continue to avoid in these pages promoting an ideal of no-conflict, but rather of alertness and security in the Lord. The strategy may be likened to navigational instruments that assure steady direction even as adjustment to unfriendly elements is required. The Lord sometimes brings us "through fire and through water" (Ps 66:12) before providing a place of refreshment, but he does, and he will.

A compass for safe passage, and not instructions for definitively ejecting and ridding ourselves of straying thoughts, may seem more like surrender than strategy: coexistence with the enemy. But we have seen wisdom here: Just as God uses elements of the fallen world, including the fallen angels (see Ephesians above), to try and perfect us, so in our *inner world* our fallen nature provides the perhaps unlikely material for our sanctification. What is at stake here is nothing short of the recovery of our lost integrity:

> For a monumental struggle against the powers of darkness pervades the whole history of man. The battle was joined from the very origins of the world and will continue until the last day, as the Lord has attested. Caught in this conflict, man is obliged to wrestle constantly if he is to cling to what is good, nor can he achieve his own integrity without great efforts and the help of God's grace.[1]

The graphic language of clinging and wrestling reveals the need for a high degree of tenacity in our moral choices. Far from whims or preferences, to cling is to hold on as counter forces seek to tear you away. Wrestling means trying to get the better of an opponent at close quarters, trying to outsmart him and anticipate moves while attempting to overpower him. Now, not every waking moment is of equal intensity, since by God's mercy the struggle admits of moments of tranquility and relief. But it is always in the background, never completely finished in this life.

Hence, as far as mental prayer goes, attempts to eradicate (that is, completely uproot) distractions may, along with being mostly futile, be surprisingly counterproductive. "To set about hunting down distractions would be to fall into their trap," says the *Catechism*,

> when all that is necessary is to turn back to our heart: for a distraction reveals to us what we are attached to, and

> this humble awareness before the Lord should awaken our preferential love for him and lead us resolutely to offer him our heart to be purified. Therein lies the battle, the choice of which master to serve.[2]

The wisdom here is as simple as it is stunning. A strategic truth emerges: Distractions or straying thoughts are like wartime intelligence about our vulnerabilities. Their attempted incursions reveal where we are weak and where we especially need the Lord to defend and strengthen us. Likewise, as the *Catechism* points out, we are regularly presented with the choice of masters. The choice reduces ultimately to two, as the Lord also says (Mt 6:24), even if the riches or "mammon" he refers to may be broadened to include anything outside of God in which we find our security.

The Carmelite spiritual writer, Fr. Gabriel of St. Mary Magdalene (1893–1953), makes a similar point about the directions into which memory spontaneously bifurcates. In his masterful and succinct overview of the doctrine of St. John of the Cross, Fr. Gabriel comments:

> We know by experience that the memory dwells more frequently on the recollections of things that we love and of those that we fear: of those that we love, because in them are determined the various aims and purposes of our lives, which are so many motives for arousing our industrious impulses; of those that we fear, because we see them as so many forces that can hinder us from attaining our goals. These are the sources of our agitations and of the infinite solicitudes that do not give peace to our spirit

> and keep us preoccupied, troubled, and at times render us quite unhappy.[3]

Another way of expressing it is that love is equivalent to attraction or conversion (literally, turning toward) or desire. What we want draws us along, whether it is something truly good for us or something that only appears good in some respect. St. Augustine speaks of how we are all drawn by our desires. Distractions in prayer, wandering thoughts throughout the day, really do reveal where our hearts are at.

A text frequently employed by the Fathers to demonstrate the force of love is the famous line from the Song of Songs: "Draw me after you, let us make haste" (1:4). Although St. Paul lists "patient" as the first quality of love, some kinds of love are not so inclined to wait it out. Where 1 Corinthians 13 famously extols the facets of holy charity, the love of attraction leaps over barriers to reach the beloved and will not heed the cautions or threats voiced by the prudent of this world, as the same Song attests:

> Upon my bed by night
> I sought him whom my soul loves;
> I sought him, but found him not;
> I called him, but he gave no answer.
> "I will rise now and go about the city,
> in the streets and in the squares;
> I will seek him whom my soul loves."
> I sought him, but found him not.
> The watchmen found me,
> as they went about in the city.

"Have you seen him whom my soul loves?"
Scarcely had I passed them,
  when I found him whom my soul loves.
I held him, and would not let him go
  until I had brought him into my mother's house,
  and into the chamber of her that conceived me.
    (Song 3:1–4)

Fear, on the other hand, is aversion to, a turning away from, some present or impending evil (real or imagined) so that we might imagine how we can escape it, or otherwise fall into sadness from its inevitability.

As we read Fr. Gabriel's words, we can immediately see ourselves reflected in them, for this is how our memory and imagination work. That we are given intelligence regarding the inclinations of our desires is plain; the work now before us is to cultivate desires more in keeping with God's will, should our spontaneous likings and aversions suggest deviation from it. But this process is not simply making acts of the will contrary to our fallen appetites. The priority, especially where our thoughts are habitually drawn to certain areas, is to ask: What good am I seeking here? In other words, what good underlies the distorted desire that plays in my imagination?

If the *Catechism* indicates that, to some extent, distractions will always be there, this does not mean they will always bother to the same degree, in kind or intensity. One very important step is to accept your own thoughts as manifesting something about you: your desires, fears, aversions, dreams. Some of them might be embarrassing, others shameful, others noble and beautiful. But under each is something fundamentally good.

Vices are disorders. This implies that there is an ordered way of going about attaining the goods that vices exploit and corrupt.

The great Benedictine spiritual writer Hubert van Zeller (1905–1984) with characteristic clarity, frames this topic of interior struggle in terms of nagging feelings of "doubt, fear, loneliness, frustration and so on." These, he says, "are not so much fought and conquered as acknowledged and transcended."[4] If transcending means getting or going beyond something, then we might wonder how we can possibly do this. Sometimes well-meaning advice is given to the angered or injured, to someone undergoing some unpleasantness, to "move on." The facile idea is that it is within the power of the one suffering to get over the problem, presumably by self-distraction: thinking about or doing other things, for example.

Sometimes people are their own worst enemy. As such, we might very well sabotage our own happiness by dwelling disproportionately on thoughts of unfair treatment, the net effect of which is to continually stir the pot of resentment. Or regarding a time of loss (of loved one, job, status, etc.) as permanently debilitating, as a state from which recovery is impossible, is another way of failing to help ourselves along the path of life. We can so mishandle suffering as to make its impact more devastating than it needs to be. This is no glib assertion, since it is always difficult to deal with losses gracefully. Life has no shortage of devastation; that is not in question. What is always in question, however, is what we do with it.

Christians have resources that nonbelievers do not have. When suffering is especially unmerited and absurd, we always have the example of the crucified Lord, "who for the joy that was set before him endured the cross, despising the shame" (Heb 12:2). Far more than a moral example, the suffering of Jesus means—is equivalent to—his love for us. So we are not only imitating Jesus by enduring trials; when we unite ourselves to him, we experience the encouragement of his love—perhaps best conceptualized as an empathy than which none is deeper. If human empathy seeks, always imperfectly, to feel the feelings and think the thoughts of another, Jesus actually did this by the Incarnation and especially in his passion. He knows what we think and feel *from the inside*, so that we don't have to explain anything to him. He knows.

Caryll Houselander summarizes Christ's unique empathy with us in extraordinary experiential language, reminiscent of Isaiah's Suffering Servant: "Christ has lived each of our lives, he has faced all our fears, suffered all our griefs, overcome all our temptations, labored in all our labors, loved in all our loves, died all our deaths."[5] There is nothing about you that Christ Jesus doesn't "get." He knows you, even the *fallen you* that you would rather hide from him and everyone else. He knows the darkness and perversion that sometimes drifts like a thick fog through your thoughts and desires. He knows how you struggle to be free. He knows how much you want to be a saint but lose courage as you repeatedly encounter your sinfulness. He comes to redeem it all.

Any one of the experiences van Zeller mentions ("doubt, fear, loneliness, frustration") can become the central theme of our preoccupations and derail further spiritual, psychological, and emotional growth. You might object at this point that the problem you are facing is not that you want to dwell on these thoughts or feelings but that you recognize them as harmful and want to stop. You want them to stop repeating, but you can't interrupt them—at least in a way that completely disperses them.

This points to a need for deeper healing. We can distract ourselves from our distractions, but we cannot heal ourselves, cannot reach to the underlying insecurities and fears that prompt unwanted thoughts. This is the work of the Holy Spirit. If we are counseled by van Zeller to "acknowledge and transcend," this is how it is done on the deepest levels. We must acknowledge the persistent thought before God with humility, with confidence that he can show us why these thoughts and not others so preoccupy us. Frequently this will require a spiritual director and/or, depending on the nature of the problem, a therapist.

Healing will happen in God's time, at his pace, to the extent he wills, because this whole process is one of growth, not of ridding ourselves of inconvenient debilities (that is, those that especially prompt us to feel weak). Weakness and vulnerability are good before God; at least St. Paul certainly thinks so: "I will all the more gladly boast of my weaknesses, that the power of Christ may rest upon me" (2 Cor 12:9). God can use our frailties for his glory, and what could be better than that? When we have sufficiently understood what our vulnerabilities teach us, we will get beyond them—not by leaving weakness behind but by not acting out of them (such as doubt, fear, loneliness, frustration, resentment, etc.). Instead, we will learn to act out of humility and love.

The unique battle of the spiritual life, to be sure, always involves our choices, our will, against what tempts and distracts us. But it is crucial to know that we are not the winners or masters as much as the recipients of redemptive healing, empowering grace. Grace enables us to transcend the tumult of thoughts and desires and find the Lord through it all, much as the apostles saw the Lord walking on the storm-tossed Sea of Galilee. They dropped their oars and took him aboard, and immediately arrived at the land to which they had been struggling to reach (see Jn 6:16–21).

It is not by thinking hard and concentrating even harder that unwanted thoughts depart, as though frightened off by our degree of seriousness. They don't care. They are perfectly capable of turning a meditation on the sorrows of Our Lady into commercial jingles or something worse. When bothered by unwanted thoughts, one of the biggest strategic mistakes we can make is, as one religious once remarked to me, "getting worked up about it."

St. Teresa of Ávila mentions in several places how having even a single good thought is not possible without God's help. In fact, despite our best efforts, sometimes it is virtually impossible to sustain good and linear thoughts. As she says regarding souls who might be relying overmuch on their own efforts:

> I don't say that they shouldn't strive carefully to remain in God's presence, but that if they can't even get a good thought, as I've mentioned elsewhere, they shouldn't kill themselves. We are useless servants, what do we think we can do?[6]

The conclusion I draw from the words of this great doctor of prayer is that our efforts at recollection, although necessary, are not decisive in the quality of our prayer, or whether prayer happens at all. Prayer is a grace. It is not an activity I initiate and sustain like a hobby, but is best conceptualized as a response to God's invitation, his knocking at our door, which we may heed by letting him in, or postpone and ignore altogether (see Rev 3:20). This understanding removes a layer of unholy stress by helping us see that were it not for God's initiative we would not even think about praying. Our part is to say yes to the invitation and strive to listen and respond as best we can.

Another holy Spaniard says:

> A Christian's struggle must be unceasing, for interior life consists in beginning and beginning again. This prevents us from proudly thinking that we are perfect already. It is inevitable that we should meet difficulties on our way. If we did not come up against obstacles, we would not be creatures of flesh and blood. We will always have passions which pull us downwards; we will always have to defend ourselves against more or less self-defeating urges.
>
> We should not be surprised to find, in our body and soul, the needle of pride, sensuality, envy, laziness and the desire to dominate others. This is a fact of life, proven by our personal experience. It is the point of departure and the normal context for winning in this intimate sport, this race toward our Father's house. . . .
>
> To begin or sustain this conflict a Christian should not wait for external signs or nice inner feelings. Interior life does not consist in feelings but in divine grace, willingness, and love.[7]

The need for beginning again does not mean that our relationship with God starts from scratch over and over. Rather it continues to develop, unevenly, just as St. Peter's relationship with Jesus included exalted moments and at least one or two occasions when Peter could barely make eye contact with the Lord. The unevenness is a concrete confirmation that the spiritual life is not constituted of what I feel about prayer, God, or liturgy, but of "divine grace, willingness, and love."

Beginning again renews that childlike simplicity that avoids picturing ourselves as so proficient, so grown-up as it were, as to be immune from the weaknesses of the flesh. We might recall the tax collector's prayer, which Our Lord proposes as an example for the rest of us:

> . . . the tax collector, standing far off, would not even lift up his eyes to heaven, but beat his breast, saying, "God, be merciful to me a sinner!" I tell you, this man went down to his house justified rather than the other; for every one who exalts himself will be humbled, but he who humbles himself will be exalted. (Lk 18:13–14)

We will always be sinners, and in this sense we will always need to keep our feet on the ground (even if God, on occasion, makes saints like Teresa to levitate), praying from square one. This means that I need to remind myself time and again that God is God and I am not. If we keep track of how often we try to control the outcomes of daily life, we will begin to give thanks for the reminders he sends, even in the form of weaknesses and failures.

The fact that little children often want to hear the same story over and over might tell us a lot about spiritual childhood in relation to God. "Tell me," we could say to the Lord, "Tell me again of the story of your mercy, of the love you have for me, of the joy you take in finding the one lost sheep, of the water that will quench my thirst, of the Bread of Life that sustains my soul." As the Lord retells his story so do we retell ours in prayer: "God, be merciful to me a sinner!" In the light of his mercies and our miseries, no other prayer makes sense. No other prayer is less prone to distraction.

ENDNOTES

1. Vatican Council II, Pastoral Constitution on the Church in the Modern World *Gaudium et Spes* (December 7, 1965), no. 37. https://www.vatican.va.

2. *Catechism*, no. 2729.

3. Gabriel of St. Mary Magdalene, *Union with God: According to St. John of the Cross*, trans. Sr. Miriam of Jesus (Carmel of Maria Regina, 1990), p. 73. Republished by Sophia Institute Press, 2019.

4. Hubert van Zeller, *The Yoke of Divine Love* (Templegate, 1957), p. 161.

5. Caryll Houselander, *The Risen Christ* (Scepter, 2010), p. 8.

6. Teresa of Ávila, *The Book of Her Life*, p. 197.

7. Josemaría Escrivá, *Christ Is Passing By* (Scepter, 2002), no. 75.

NINE

The Enemy Within: The Problem of Self-Sabotage

Before continuing with a subset of the war described in the previous chapter (that is, the particular battle for purity of heart), a shorter chapter on self-sabotage compels itself. We unreflectively thwart our own efforts with relative ease. "I know, I know" is the mantra of the self-inflicting person, knowing the rightness of self-improvement but resisting the implementation of strategy. The car remains on a hydraulic lift, but the rubber never hits the road.

This chapter is about things we don't know but nevertheless believe, and act on, with the assumed conviction of their truth. An earlier reference to automatic thoughts, and the tacit core beliefs generating them, deserves some fleshing out in the light of the kind of warfare we are advocating. If we build with one hand and tear down with the other, we will continue to sabotage our very good intentions and risk quitting in light of our patently fruitless efforts. Sometimes the cliché "Work smarter, not harder" also applies to the spiritual life.

Our first thoughts about anything are normally accepted uncritically. Most of the time this is probably not a bad thing. Spending a disproportionate amount of time in deliberation is not helpful in most of the day's decisions. But adequate self-knowledge requires an awareness of the contents of consciousness, the entire spectrum of thoughts, from the wise and noble to the foolish and selfish. We need to know not only what we think but why we think what we think.

The practice of the examen advocated by St. Ignatius of Loyola is comprehensive. It goes beyond the examination of conscience, largely a moral inventory of failings, and scans the entire plane of consciousness. This amounts to discerning not only where we have gone wrong, but more positively, also knowing how God is communicating with us, attracting us to the good, dissuading us from evil, consoling or correcting us. Habituating ourselves to this mode of thinking opens up the ordinariness of the day into a series of encounters with the Lord, with the unceasing give-and-take characteristic of any good relationship.

As we drew parallels in an earlier chapter between spiritual recollection and cognitive distance (that is, putting some space between ourselves and our thought patterns to discern their validity), now we provide some material for that discernment from a more psychological point of view. Aaron Beck developed a list of cognitive distortions commonly associated with depression, and over the course of decades these have found broader application in areas of anxiety, phobic reactions, and other strong and debilitating responses to stressors.

Different versions of these thoughts with various wordings are found in workbooks for depression, anxiety, and obsessive-compulsiveness. Most originate with Beck or Albert Ellis, and others have been added by theoreticians and practitioners over the years. Admittedly, the introduction of these cognitive distortions takes us deeper into psychotherapy than a book of this nature is designed to go. Yet for those unfamiliar with these categories of unhelpful thoughts, sometimes simply mentioning them can spark a minor revelation.

An additional layer of introduction may help illustrate the type of thoughts under discussion here. Catholics are at ease with dogma as a theological term denoting a revealed and therefore unchanging and unchangeable doctrine of the Faith. It is the nature of a revealed truth to be constant throughout whatever changes may occur in human thought and history. The tenets of the approved creedal statements of the Church (for example, the Apostles' Creed, Athanasian, and Nicene Creeds) represent dogmatic statements.

Yet criticism of "dogmatism" in any context, religious or otherwise, is common. To be called dogmatic is derogatory in modern parlance. However, we shouldn't believe for a second that anyone is without dogmas altogether. It's just a matter of which ones you choose to hold, even if you would bristle at calling them dogmas. Those who say they don't believe in any unchanging truth have succeeded in making a dogma out of relativism. Whenever a principle of thought is adduced as a lens or an interpretive key for understanding the world, something approaching the dogmatic has been established as an unquestionable way of seeing reality.

A certain form of dogmatism is pathological, and has nothing to do with adhering to the fact of the Incarnation or belief in the Redemption. In this alternative and diminished sense of the word, people have within their interpretive outlook an inflexible, stark, un-nuanced way of seeing the world. The origin of the distorted outlook may be found as early as childhood, where parents and elders may have inculcated the problematic attitudes. The perspective may be prejudicial to self or to others, or may idealize self and others in a highly unrealistic way.

On some level it is easier to see things without qualification. Qualification equals making distinctions, and making distinctions equals laboring through the reasoning process, and reasoning means thinking correctly. And that can be hard work. The more biased we are for or against self, others, the world, and so on, the harder it can be to discern degrees of goodness and badness. Yet justice and charity demand the discernment. The health of our cognitions, and emotions, demands it no less.

Listings of common cognitive distortions can be found in any theoretical or practical treatment of cognitive behavioral therapy, whether print or online.[1] Although these particular types of thoughts are normally not considered in books of spirituality, getting to know the contents of our thoughts, whether healthy or dysfunctional, can only be an asset to every dimension of life. Sometimes people who seek spiritual direction think in unhealthy patterns, and problems they might attribute to external causes may instead be a matter of perceptual distortion. In any case, someone external to us can help assess the filters through which we see ourselves, others, and even God himself.

An inexhaustive list of some common distortions:

1. Black and white thinking: Sometimes called "dichotomous" thinking, people are judged sharply as good or bad, useful or useless. Situations are optimal or dismal. There are only winners and losers. No grey areas are considered. This can lead to *labeling*, another distortion, which refuses to consider the facets of self and others: I'm stupid; he's a weirdo; she's a drama queen.
2. All or nothing thinking: Sometimes called "absolutizing," our and others' actions and daily events are characterized as "never" or "always" occurring, always good or always bad. Someone may think they "always sound stupid" whenever they speak in public.
3. Catastrophizing: A type of pessimism that habitually imagines the worst possible outcome in any given situation. If I must drive somewhere, I will definitely get into a horrible car accident before reaching my destination.
4. Overgeneralizing: Taking one instance and generalizing it to all possible instances. If I felt flustered when someone asked a question I wasn't prepared to answer, I might tell myself that I never know what to say when someone asks me a question.
5. Emotional reasoning: How I feel about something reliably reflects its status. I feel like today is going to be a good (or bad) day, and therefore it will be.

6. Magical thinking: Drawing cause-and-effect relationships between unrelated things. Washing your car makes it rain.
7. Jumping to conclusions (also known as fortune-telling or mind reading): Hastily basing judgments on inadequate evidence. Imagining I know what another is thinking ("He must think I'm stupid") or anticipating disaster because bad things are destined to happen to me.
8. Disqualifying the positive: Ignoring positive feedback while focusing on a minor criticism. Also occurs when evaluating a positive comment as someone "just being nice" (that is to say, insincere in their compliment).
9. Magnification and minimization: Either my accomplishments mean everything or they mean nothing. I am either extremely important or utterly insignificant. No normal, no ordinary, no more or less exists.
10. "Should" statements: Without ignoring ideals, yet one expects that people and circumstances should always be a certain way. Often, nothing is ever good enough. This distortion considers the normal flaws and inconsistencies of daily life as unacceptable aberrations. St. Teresa, as we have seen, continually cautions her sisters against expecting too perfect a focus in their prayer life: "I should be praying better." It's so vague as to forbid practical steps to improvement.

The takeaway here is that although we may not be aware of our own distorted thinking, we should be aware that it might be affecting our interior lives to a greater or lesser degree. Everyone entertains cognitive distortions from time to time.

We have days when everything looks dark to us and we feel like complete failures. The point is to recognize when we are skewing our perceptions volitionally by biases against self or others, so that we can bring them to the Lord for healing.

> Why do you see the speck that is in your brother's eye, but do not notice the log that is in your own eye? Or how can you say to your brother, "Let me take the speck out of your eye," when there is the log in your own eye? You hypocrite, first take the log out of your own eye, and then you will see clearly to take the speck out of your brother's eye. (Mt 7:3–5)

What I identified as a type of dogmatism earlier finds a match in cognitive distortions, insofar as they are practically regarded as certitudes. But whereas dogmas of the Faith bring us deeper into reality, these negative filters create distance between self and others, between self and God. They turn our prayer time into a cognitive walk through a room full of funhouse mirrors.

ENDNOTES

1. Francisco Insa, *The Formation of Affectivity: A Christian Approach* (Saint Augustine's Press, 2023), pp. 282–283. Fr. Insa comments on seventeen cognitive distortions as enumerated in C. L. Yurica and R. A. DiTomasso, "Cognitive Distortions," in A. Freeman et al. (eds.), *Encyclopedia of Cognitive Behavioral Therapy* (Springer, 2004), pp. 117–121.

TEN
Fighting for Love

If the *Catechism* speaks frankly of "The Battle of Prayer,"[1] it tellingly employs the same language in presenting the virtue of chastity as "The Battle for Purity."[2] An important follow-up to chapter eight is this particular battlefield, which in the last generation or two has sprung up practically everywhere. For very many people this is *the* struggle vis-à-vis the imagination and memory.

St. Josemaría wisely counsels remote defense as a safeguard for this almost ubiquitous struggle, and in this chapter we will consider what types of remote defenses are best suited to building the virtue of purity, in a culture where it is continually contested and undermined.

> That supernatural way of conducting yourself is a real military strategy.
>
> You carry on the war—the daily battles of your interior life—in positions far from the main walls of your fortress.

> And the enemy comes to meet you there: in your small mortification, in your daily prayer, in your orderly work, in your plan of life. And only with difficulty does he get close to the otherwise easily-scaled battlements of your citadel. And if he does, he arrives exhausted.[3]

By the time the enemy reaches you, St. Josemaría imaginatively implies, he has had to negotiate several barricades, and so is weakened to the point of negligibility. Preventative measures, in other words, render us less and less reachable by temptation. It is not that we become impervious but that we have employed enough reasonable safeguards as to not leave ourselves vulnerable to preventable attacks. Some battles we walk into because of a lack of foresight or prudence. Others are sprung upon us despite our best efforts. But the habit of self-protection renders even these less potent than if we were simply negligent.

More broadly, St. Josemaría advocates order over chaos to help bring greater intentionality to our daily life—which, if it operates according to a plan, is additionally enriched by meaning. When our lives are fettered by avoidable chaos, our stress levels rise and the likelihood we will cope badly increases exponentially. Address the stress, in other words, and you find less urge for quick relief. If we live and work according to a plan, rewards are twofold: first, the sense of accomplishment at finished tasks; second, the freedom to treat ourselves to something truly recreating and relaxing afterward.

In the absence of order, the imagination coasts more easily to dubious daydreams and fantasies: "Generally, letting your imagination loose is a waste of time, and, if it is not controlled, it opens the door to a whole string of voluntary temptations."[4] The point is that stress not directed constructively to the task at hand, a task requiring some immediate intensity of effort and energy, is like a foreign body your emotional immune system wants to expel by any means necessary. And it's not too picky about what it selects to distract you.

The importance of new and truer conceptional categories reemerges here. The imagination that possesses only a limited, worldly frame of reference will have nowhere to go when disturbing thoughts intrude. A mind having been trained in biblical and spiritual ways of perception, however, will find empathy from Jesus and the saints, a Sacred Heart that loves us in our struggle, and saints who have been embattled exactly as we are.

Order is a key component for maintaining a productive life, since disorders foment tension and create an environment where everything overwhelms and nothing is ever really finished. But one can create an order of sorts in daily life with agendas and schedules without accounting for the soul's greatest need: love. And this is where impurity meets its most formidable adversary.

Recall the house Jesus describes as "swept and put in order" but altogether devoid of life, of love, of anything substantial (Lk 11:25). A vacant house—an empty soul—is vulnerable to all kinds of infestations, break-ins, occupations. In the Lord's teaching a colony of demons happily moves in to possess the place. Order, then, is an irreplaceable structure for both functionality and flourishing in life and love; but the framework needs to be filled.

It is too simplistic and inaccurate to say that lust/impurity is a problem isolated from general relational health and other interpersonal issues, as we have mentioned. Many nevertheless simply want the thoughts to go away after they have decided to turn away from pornography and lustful behavior. The thoughts linger and tend to recur, unsurprisingly, especially under conditions of stress.

The *Catechism*'s analogy between battle and self-mastery, battle and prayer, reveals both purity and prayer as among the most desirable and difficult goods to cultivate, each requiring an ongoing care to both protect and make fruitful. Each is ordered toward a deep and intimate relationship that may only be fully enjoyed when one is free enough to love. And love is never proved to be free and genuine unless it has been tested by its adversaries: selfishness, cowardice, and sensuality—all of which thwart the sacrifice that is at the heart of love.

Prayer, like purity, is ordered toward relationship. A heart is kept pure for the sake of loving others well—not in a self-centered, exploitative way, but as a gift of self. Purity of heart is not equivalent to naiveté or to ignorance of the affective and sexual dimensions of life, much less a fear of them. Where fear dominates, repression has likely stifled healthy psychosexual development. Where sexuality has not been allowed to develop and be integrated into our overall emotional and affective life, it might camouflage as a kind of purity or innocence, but it is neither. It is a stunted part that prevents real self-giving and intimacy in relationships.

Purity is cultivated for the sake of loving with greater intensity and intimacy—so that when we love another, our love is felt by another as love (put another way, as an affirming gift). We can tell the discrepancy when someone professes love but who takes advantage of trust or passivity to exploit. We feel used, not loved.

The purity of our prayer, purified of as much distraction and daydreaming as we can manage, is also a battle fought for the sake of relationship. The *Catechism* asks "Against whom?" do we conduct our offensive, and answers: "Against ourselves and against the wiles of the tempter who does all he can to turn man away from prayer, away from union with God."[5] Union equals love, and union with God is the final goal of all prayer, whether prayer is liturgical, private, vocal, or mental. Union with God means our wills are united; our relationship is one of love.

These relational principles are crucial to understanding the end for which we cultivate a pure heart and try, with humble perseverance, to turn away from tempting thoughts. Understanding how these thoughts operate is no less important, especially with respect to their duration, persistence, and the ambiguous moral quality they seem to possess.

Years before his election to the See of Peter, St. John Paul II wrote *Love and Responsibility*, a work that beautifully explores the deeply interpersonal meaning of human sexuality as designed by God, while also helpfully identifying the challenges of such a powerful biological and affective force. Among the recognized difficulties is the lingering nature of the feelings incited by spontaneous sexual thoughts and their morality. People often don't know if they've consented, or to what extent they've consented.

I normally tell people that, in general, God does not want us to have such a clear window into our moral life. He wants us to trust him more than our own moral rectitude. Some people can't stand that, but it's true. Not all of our moral actions may be clearly assessed with infallible certainty, which is why we might preface our confessions sometimes with "I think" or "I'm not sure if." In such cases all we have to do is be completely sincere and humble, and know that God is pleased with our willingness to confess even what we're not sure of.

In this lengthy but extremely enlightening passage, St. John Paul II identifies the problem of the "boundaries of sin" in our moral actions, while also helping us understand the feelings attendant on sexual provocations in the imagination. Understanding how unwanted thoughts of a sexual nature should be judged and handled will take us a long way in dealing with them without undue anxiety.

> In practice there is here a problem which some people sometimes find quite difficult, *the problem of the boundaries of sin*. Objectively, the dividing line is drawn by acts of will, by conscious and voluntary assent of the will. But there are people who have difficulty in identifying the border line. Concupiscence in human beings has its own dynamic, by which it endeavours to become a conscious desire, an act of will, and hence anyone who lacks the proper power of discrimination may easily take as an act of will what is only the prompting of the senses and of carnal desire. A sensual reaction follows its own course for a time, thanks to the dynamic inherent in concupiscence, even when the will not only does not assent but expressly opposes it. An act of will directed against a sensual impulse does not generally produce any

> immediate result. In its own (psychological) sphere a sensual reaction generally runs its full course even if it meets emphatic opposition in the sphere of the will. No-one can demand of himself either that he should experience no sensual reactions at all, or that they should immediately yield just because the will does not consent, or even because it declares itself definitely "against." This is a point of great importance to those who seek to practice continence. There is a difference between "not wanting" and "not feeling," "not experiencing."
>
> It follows then that in analysing the structure of sin we must not attach too much importance to sensuality as such nor yet to concupiscence. A spontaneous sensual reaction, a carnal reflex, is not in itself a sin, nor will it become sin, unless the will leads the way.[6]

Respecting the natural trajectory of our feelings, especially the ones of greater intensity, fosters patience, the virtue so essential in so many domains of life. We avoid getting worked up or frustrated because, after all, we are human and human emotions do not turn on and off by a command of the will. This does not mean that letting them run wild is the only alternative but that gentle care is required in reeling them in, submitting them to reason and acting according to virtue.

Because our feelings spontaneously react to our perceptions and the meaning we give to our perceptions, we should employ a suitable strategy in redirecting them toward truly good objects. If alluring and seductive images oppress the soul, fighting fire with fire, like with like, may be the most effective strategy: Images that distort and exploit sexuality should be replaced by images that inspire heroic love; seductive narratives should be replaced by readings that motivate the pursuit of holiness by taking us out of ourselves in service.

If you were raised in an environment where any talk of sex was practically taboo, and therefore even healthy education and formation in sexuality was nonexistent, then some remedial education is likely in order. It doesn't matter how old you are. Adults who have never received adequate formation in human sexuality will always retain a certain curiosity and immaturity about it. In a good sense, the mystery needs to be taken out of it; its forbidden nature needs replacing with knowledge of it as a normal and privileged part of married love, yet far from the most important expression of it. Any fear regarding sexuality, especially the feelings it inspires, should be corrected with the truth of its goodness as willed by God. This entire process is a part of the larger project of affective maturity and emotional integration. Mishandling of the sexual dimension of our affectivity cannot be left uncorrected. Inner peace only comes when all of our emotions and appetites rest in their proper place, with none banished as unacceptable.

Over time the imagery that once exercised such a tempting force will emerge more and more clearly as a disgusting counterfeit. Even so, we shouldn't be surprised if occasionally we are still tempted by the disgusting, but neither should we shame ourselves by thinking that, after all this time, how could we still find such and such alluring? Fallen people will always have fallen desires. Humility is not surprised to find them there.

We can tell from the foregoing that the contrary of lust is not absence of feeling, absence of affection. It is rightly ordered love. Lust is simply a cheap and exploitative version of sexual love, which God made to unite husband and wife in the self-gift characterized by vulnerability and trust. Lust possesses neither of these interpersonal qualities, nor any wholesome interpersonal qualities at all.

St. John Henry Newman describes how divine action converts the soul from sinful to saintly, showing how the human powers misused in sinning are the same faculties God uses to bring someone to salvation, especially the will to love:

> He violates in nothing that original constitution of mind which He gave to man: He treats him as man; He leaves him the liberty of acting this way or that; He appeals to all his powers and faculties, to his reason, to his prudence, to his moral sense, to his conscience: He rouses his fears as well as his love; He instructs him in the depravity of sin, as well as in the mercy of God; but still, on the whole, the animating principle of the new life, by which it is both kindled and sustained, is the flame of charity. This only is strong enough to destroy the old Adam, to dissolve the tyranny of habit, to quench the fires of concupiscence, and to burn up the strongholds of pride.[7]

The concluding image of the flame really makes the point: The answer to a destructive fire is not no-fire. Rather it is a fire that warms and motivates goodness. The flame is made of the same stuff, but the fuel it consumes has changed. Love misspent, love disordered, can become pure and strong where the objects of love are noble. The process by which love is purified, by which the mind and heart redirect their focus onto "whatever is true, whatever is honorable, whatever is just, whatever is pure, whatever is lovely" (Phil 4:8), is essentially one of crowding out the inadequate with the superior. Displacing the defective objects of our attention with ones that ennoble is the crafty strategy that gradually cleanses the imagination of troubling and tempting images. Or, as St. John of the Cross puts it, we need the "enkindling of another, better love" to override the pull of the inferior, disordered ones.[8]

To stop consuming obscene materials is a huge step in the battle for purity, but since the conflict continues in memory and feelings, replacement is necessary. Jordan Peterson makes the same point in discussing alcoholism and other addictive behaviors with Matt Fradd: "No one ever quits anything; they replace it with something better."[9] In this context Peterson cites "religious transformation" as "the most reliable cure" for alcoholism and its equivalents, a conclusion supported by decades of research and the lived experience of many.[10] Bl. Fulton J. Sheen mirrors Peterson's point while supplying the content for the transformation:

> It does no good to tell people to stop doing certain things, unless they can be given something else to do that they will care for more. An alcoholic will not be persuaded to give up the liquor he loves unless he is made to love something else. For evil can never be thrown out; it must be crowded out. When finally a Perfect Love is found, there is less adhesion to other things. . . .[11]

What differentiates the religious "cure" from all other contenders is its status as the highest possible goal you can aim at.

If lust is the problem, if relationships are unhealthy, then turning to the Lord and the Blessed Mother lifts your mind and heart far above the miserable distortions of love and intimacy this fallen world continually tries to pawn off on us. After we die, the world, the flesh, and the devil will still be up to their same old stratagems, trying to allure souls into believing lies about love. Once we've awakened to the deception in our own lifetime we can begin to taste a love that gives itself in sacrifice for us and fires us to do the same. This is what Jesus does for us. This is what devotion to the Blessed Virgin accomplishes. As Newman beautifully says, "It is the boast of the Catholic Religion, that it has the gift of making the young heart chaste; and why is this, but that it gives us Jesus Christ for our food, and Mary for our nursing Mother?"[12]

The point is ultimately very simple, but in the often-discouraging return journey of purity, which seems to be an impossible project of forgetting, people encounter points when nothing seems to work. Prayer appears to be doomed to continual intrusions, with sin ever "couching at the door" (Gn 4:7). Here again, patience and humility are the watchwords. We must accept the fact of having misused our minds and commit ourselves to the undoing of the damage by the grace of meditation, recognizing that contemplating the true, good, and beautiful will stir our hearts to love what our hearts were made to love: the God who is Love.

Again, Bishop Sheen paints the picture more realistically and positively than any I can imagine. Our work is not only or mainly remedial, which is a discouraging idea from any angle, but a positive effort to live in "the climate of Divine Love."

Here again is the language of crowding out and replacement, particularly in the context of meditative prayer:

> Meditation effects far more profound changes in us than resolutions to "do better"; we cannot keep evil thoughts out of our minds unless we put good ones in their place. Supernature, too, abhors a vacuum. In meditation one does not *drive* sin out of his life; he *crowds* it out with the love of God and neighbor. Our lives do not then depend on the principle of avoiding sin, which is a tiresome job, but on living constantly in the climate of Divine Love. Meditation, in a word, prevents defeat where defeat is final: in the mind. In that silence where God is, false desires steal away. If we meditate before we go to bed, our last thought at night will be our first thought in the morning. There will be none of that dark brown feeling with which some men face a meaningless day; and in its place will be the joy of beginning another morning of work in Christ's Name.[13]

I have repeated this point throughout this chapter not only because pedagogy suggests it but because the process is fundamental to reclaiming our minds and hearts for Christ. The image of the ordered but empty house haunted anew, the inability of people to "just stop" doing the vicious actions that keep them in bonds, the frustration and even despair that people encounter trying to break free—all of these coalesce in the basic process of occupying our minds and hearts with something we love more than the activity we now hate, yet evidently cannot stop doing.

Isn't this another way of saying, "You shall love the Lord your God with all your heart, and with all your soul, and with all your strength, and with all your mind" (Lk 10:27)? Where the "all" is divided up into competing parts, integration is lacking and the stress of the conflict continues to tire and weaken the soul. Wanting to have everything, to serve God and mammon without a negative outcome, we still end up with one thing dominant and everything else subservient. This is beyond theoretical; it is the reality of love's hierarchy in the soul. Something has to be on top. You cannot have two "number ones": "No servant can serve two masters; for either he will hate the one and love the other, or he will be devoted to the one and despise the other" (Lk 16:13). Much less can one serve three, four, or more masters.

Linking this back to prayer, the great Teresa is once again our go-to:

> For if the will is not occupied and love has nothing present with which to be engaged, the soul is left as though without support or exercise, and the solitude and dryness is very troublesome, and the battle with one's thoughts extraordinary.[14]

What constitutes "extraordinary" for St. Teresa must be great indeed, especially where love is so strong and focused. But the principle is identical to all we've been saying here: unless love focuses itself on a truly worthy object, our thoughts will keep fishing around for something better. Even more in line with the gospel parables, until we've located the pearl of great price or the treasure buried in the otherwise nondescript field, the quest will continue. We'll keep digging around and perhaps risk lassitude over time.

Once found, point of sale has been reached. Inscribed on the pearl, graven on the treasure, is: "Sell all for me."

ENDNOTES

1. *Catechism*, no. 2725.
2. *Catechism*, no. 2520.
3. Escrivá, *The Way*, no. 307.
4. Escrivá, *Furrow*, no. 135.
5. *Catechism*, no. 2725.
6. Karol Wojtyla (John Paul II), *Love and Responsibility* (Ignatius Press, 1993), p. 162.
7. John Henry Newman, "Purity and Love," in *Discourses Addressed to Mixed Congregations* (London: Longmans, Green, 1899), pp. 71–72.
8. John of the Cross, *The Ascent of Mount Carmel*, in *The Collected Works of St. John of the Cross*, p. 151. Special thanks to Fr. Daniel Chowning, OCD, for this reference.
9. Matt Fradd, host, *Pints with Aquinas*, podcast, episode 464, "Atheism, Climate Change, & Marriage Advice" (Jordan Peterson), May 13, 2024, 55:00.
10. Fradd, 56:19.
11. Fulton J. Sheen, *Lift Up Your Heart: A Guide to Spiritual Peace* (Image Books, 1955), p. 250.
12. John Henry Newman, "Discourse 18. On the Fitness of the Glories of Mary," in *Discourses Addressed to Mixed Congregations*, p. 376.
13. Sheen, *Lift Up Your Heart*, pp. 197-198.
14. Teresa of Ávila, *The Book of Her Life*, p. 68.

ELEVEN

Mind over Matter: The Ghosts of Shame

Put to rest and banish forever the multi-
headed ghosts of secret shame which attack
like pirates in their vulgar ways.
—St. Gregory of Narek[1]

Visiting the Skid Row area of Los Angeles on one occasion I chatted pleasantly with Ted, a homeless man who had lifted the flap of his tent to receive some of the food and supplies we were offering. It was nighttime, late November and cold, cold even for Los Angeles. Before leaving him I said, "Well, I hope it's not too cold for you in there." Tapping a finger to his head, Ted quickly replied, "Mind over matter," and smiled. It sounded like something Hamlet tells his hapless friends, Rosencrantz and Guildenstern: "There is nothing either good or bad, but thinking makes it so." Is the mind really that powerful?

We have reflected much on the power, character, and accuracy of our thoughts with respect to our prayer life, and indeed life in general. Our thoughts do not construct reality, but they do often determine how we perceive and feel about reality. As we have noted, this fact alone takes us far in both understanding and managing our thought processes, whether we are occupied in prayer or in other things. But understanding and managing is not the same as healing. Healing is a divine work, especially when experienced at the deepest and most remote levels of our being.

We reintroduce healing here because whenever a part of us is diseased, it draws our attention and preoccupies us, and our thinking cannot easily rise above it. Reforming our thoughts is a pointless endeavor if a wound is festering. The unsound tree cannot bear good fruit (see Mt 7:18), indicating that a root-level soundness is demanded of the disciple. Prayer, in the end, is not primarily a matter of thinking but of loving.

Healing is here conceptualized according to its biblical and theological meanings: not primarily that of the body (by no means a negligible gift), but rather that of the soul. "[Jesus'] healings were signs of the coming of the Kingdom of God. They announced a more radical healing: the victory over sin and death through his Passover."[2] The healings Jesus performs in the Gospels are certainly acts of great mercy to those "sick with various diseases" (Mk 1:34), as well as to those demonically possessed. But the bodily healings are never meant to stop in the flesh; their purpose is to turn the soul to the Lord, to reconcile the individual with God. Reconciliation and reintegration of the soul are inextricably connected. Physical healings demonstrate that link.

As God brings healing to the soul, normally not an overnight process, we might still feel leashed by the past. Hence, perhaps nothing tests the notion of "mind over matter" in our prayer life like persistent, recurring memories of past sins, mistakes, and missed opportunities. Leave the mind idle for a second and the vacuum fills up immediately with the same old things: desires, fears, fantasies, grievances, guilt, and God knows what else. Especially hazardous as we strive for spiritual progress is facing our willful negligences, stupidities, arrogance—all of the bad qualities to which we once gave free play and that now mortify us. Few describe this phenomenon more incisively than van Zeller:

> Our memory shows us a list of half-forgotten infidelities; our imagination builds up a lurid picture of our guilt. Reason reproaches us for having so consistently acted independently of its light; the will has no explanation to offer for the way in which we have misused true liberty and followed the attraction of our lower nature.[3]

We might be especially susceptible to this frame of mind after a conversion experience. After turning to the Lord, thoughts almost inevitably begin to rush upon the soul: "I can't believe I used to do that. What was I thinking?" Images of yourself at your worst intrude upon your newfound piety, calling it all into question. *You used to tell lies to get what you wanted. You exploited the vulnerability of others. You indulged all your appetites thinking you knew what the good life was all about. You seduced and were seduced. You thought you had the world on a string. You were the center of everything and made others pay the price if they got in your way. Your conscience warned you, and you did it all anyway. And now here you are, acting pious.*

Such thoughts occur not only in the wake of conversion: They also attend the deepening of our prayer life, which develops in tandem with ongoing conversion. The discrepancy between present insight compared to the relative indifference of the past is certainly a part of spiritual growth, just as insight normally accompanies each successive stage of life. Perspective changes. Wisdom accrues. Regret and embarrassment are normal.

However, the spiritual life might better express itself as it passes through stages of maturity with a humble recognition of its developmental nature. Instead of cringing at our immature self—easy to do—we could reflect: "I do believe that I used to think, speak, and act the way I did, because Christ was either not at the center of my life or not as central as he should have been. It all makes sense." If the old life without Christ was that satisfying, he would not have bothered to become man, die, and rise to give us a new one. The New Testament urges us to esteem this newness of life: "Therefore, if any one is in Christ, he is a new creation; the old has passed away, behold, the new has come" (2 Cor 5:17).

In the passage cited above, van Zeller paints an uncompromising picture: We cannot pray from the depths of the heart and *not* expect truth to convict us of our failures, and failures recalled normally occasion the regret that feeds into the experience of shame. Shame might be the unforeseen outcropping of spiritual growth, so it needs to be understood lest its appearance paralyze future progress. Owing to popular usage, shame likewise requires analysis at several levels.

Shame, from a psychological point of view, is commonly understood as more or less global self-rejection. You could call it self-hatred or despising of self, to the point where hope for self-betterment is extinguished. It's not that I presently think I'm no good; it's that I believe I will never be good, that I am incapable of being good, that I am worthless and unworthy of anyone's esteem or love. If this spirit palls over your soul, your prayer life will lack the necessary ingredients of hope and joy in the Lord, not to mention confidence and trust. Why would God, or anyone, want to hear what you have to say if you can't even tolerate yourself? Prayer cannot survive in this inhospitable climate. Against this practical despair, Pope Benedict XVI asserted with refreshing simplicity:

> When no one listens to me any more, God still listens to me. When I can no longer talk to anyone or call upon anyone, I can always talk to God. When there is no longer anyone to help me deal with a need or expectation that goes beyond the human capacity for hope, he can help me.[4]

The reference to hope here is deliberate. The theological virtues undergird our prayer life; indeed our prayer is an expression of the degree to which faith, hope, and love are alive and active in our souls.

If the tendency of shame is to withdraw self from others as unworthy, as an object of disgust, then the self-rejected person needs to get acquainted with the type of people Jesus healed on a regular basis. The possessed man who self-identifies as "Legion," for example, was known to howl continually while cutting and bruising himself with stones (see Mk 5:5). Now, he was not fully responsible for the self-harm, since the demons were tormenting him. But just consider what type of spirit drives the shame that makes someone want to break the bathroom mirror, cut or otherwise harm themselves, tune out with drugs, and the like. There is real pain here, aggravated in part by unseen enemies who want all of us to join them in perfect and perpetual despair. This type of shame has nothing to do with humility or virtue whatsoever.

Shame, however, bears a more technical meaning that shows its proper place in our emotional repertoire. St. Thomas Aquinas characterizes shame ("shamefacedness") as a fear of doing something beneath human dignity or having done something disgraceful and having it exposed, or again, appearing before others in an undignified way. The Latin phrase *infra dig.*, an abbreviation of *infra dignitatem* (beneath one's dignity), reveals the cause of shame as a disgraceful act one would understandably wish to keep concealed. Aquinas explains:

> Now shamefacedness regards fault in two ways. In one way a man refrains from vicious acts through fear of reproach: in another way a man while doing a disgraceful deed avoids the public eye through fear of reproach. In the former case, according to Gregory of Nyssa, we speak of a person "blushing," in the latter we say that he is "ashamed." Hence he says that "the man who is ashamed acts in secret, but he who blushes fears to be disgraced."[5]

Echoing Aquinas, St. John Paul II observed in his Theology of the Body discourses that "A certain fear always belongs to the essence of shame."[6] The fear considered by the Pontiff was that of Adam and Eve after the Fall, when they hid from

God and from each other. This fear continues to characterize us in the umpteenth generation after our first parents, and it is not necessarily wrong or unhealthy. As long as it is understood not as wholesale self-rejection but as a reasonable apprehension over degrading behavior, then shame can operate as a helpful preventative against, for example, lust, gluttony, rage, or other forms of undignified conduct. In other words, if public exposure is the only brake on bad actions, then let it serve its purpose: an impetus to self-restraint and better behavior.

In this context we can understand Pope Francis's homiletic musings on shame as a . . . *grace*. Surprising? He even concludes the following Lenten homily with an exhortation to pray for it:

> When I recognise that I have sinned, that I have not prayed well, and I feel this in my heart, a sense of shame comes to us: "I am ashamed of having done this. I ask your pardon with shame." And shame for our sins is a grace; we must ask for it: "Lord, may I be ashamed." A person who has lost his shame loses his moral judgment, and loses respect for others. He is shameless. The same happens with God: "Shame belongs to us, righteousness belongs to you." Shame belongs to us. "Ours the look of shame we wear today," he [Daniel] continues, "to our kings, our princes, our ancestors, because we have sinned against you." . . . When we have not only the recollection, the memory of the sins we have committed, but also the sense of shame, this touches God's heart and He responds with mercy. The journey that leads toward God's mercy consists of shame for the bad, for the evil things we have

> done. In this way, when I go to confession, I will say not only the list of sins, but also the feelings of confusion, of shame for having done this to a God so good, so merciful, so just.
>
> Let us ask today for the grace of shame: to be ashamed of our sins. May the Lord grant this grace to all of us.[7]

Insofar as the emotional expression of shame leads the soul into despair, it is to be rejected outright as a temptation. It is part self-pity, part reality, and (likely) part demonic interference. If no reality or truth were present in the feeling, it wouldn't get any traction on us to begin with. The fact is we are weak, are sinful, and have done regrettable things. And we continue to do them. Any of these facts could sink the soul into a morass of discouragement.

Saints who were once unfaithful or indifferent to the call of grace ever grappled with this discrepancy between their past life and renewed life in the Lord. Saints Paul, Augustine, Margaret of Cortona, Teresa of Ávila, and Charles de Foucauld are just a handful that come to mind of holy people who rubbed their eyes at their remembrance of things past, finding their former unresponsiveness pitiable and unconceivable. But they did not obsess over the (happy) incongruity. Rather they came to understand mercy as the ultimate reality, the ultimate explanation, against which even our greatest sins have nothing worthwhile to say.

It's not that Jesus reassured them with "It wasn't so bad; don't worry," or "Don't take it all so seriously." All sin is bad and, to varying degrees, serious. We don't help ourselves in the moral life by convincing ourselves that we haven't done wrong, especially serious wrong. Some can't handle the mere idea that they could have stooped to do something disgraceful and cowardly, let alone face the consequences. But we do not and cannot stop there.

It is one thing to meditate on such Gospel scenes as the woman taken in adultery and make every effort to feel the woman's shame and desperation. It is quite another thing to be, yourself, ashamed and desperate. To feel these feelings first-hand, without the aid of the imagination, without the artificial context of meditation, this changes the story altogether. Or to see the sinful woman weeping over the feet of Jesus and drying them with her hair and to think it a beautiful and dramatic spectacle . . . versus being the weeping sinner yourself, not knowing what else to do but cry while awkwardly using your tears to bathe the Lord's feet. You are oblivious to the spectacle you're creating because it's not an act. It's your salvation. It's your plea for forgiveness.

Carl Jung, the influential psychoanalyst, aligns a sense of guilt with a patient's wholeness. He arrives at a Christian paradox from the blind side, as it were, since although an admirer of Catholicism he was not in any sense an orthodox believer. Wholeness, he says, cannot be achieved unless people accept the darkest part of themselves, what he calls "the blackest shadow,"[8] an expression integral to his conception of the human psyche. A certain integration results from facing and accepting our fallen selves and the inevitable wickedness to which we are prone. In their writings we find the saints speaking very frankly not only about how bad they have been but how capable they are of the worst. If even Our Lord refers in passing to the wickedness of his disciples (see Lk 11:13), then we must reckon with a part of ourselves capable of being a Judas.

Recognizing our bad tendencies and evil deeds does not mean making peace with them. Coexistence is not the slogan of a Christian soul, "For what partnership have righteousness and iniquity? Or what fellowship has light with darkness" (2 Cor 6:14)? Acknowledgment is an act of humble self-awareness, but is not the final conclusion. The moral wrestling alluded to earlier proves where our hearts stand right now, and it is this that helps push shame into the background.

True, we may have chosen badly and done reprehensible things even as recently as the last hour. But those closest to God, the saints, continually tell us that we can start anew at each moment. In fact, we must begin again in each moment, trusting not in our own rectitude but in the Lord's infinite mercy. We keep returning to mercy as the antidote to shame, and we will never cease making this journey. A pithy saying from the Desert Fathers shows how resilient hope can and needs to be: "Abba Moses asked Abba Silvanus, 'Can a man lay a new foundation every day?' The old man said, 'If he works hard, he can lay a new foundation at every moment.'"[9]

The answer to our problem of shame and a guilty conscience when we have done wrong is here. The answer is not to minimize the wrong we have done but to maximize the mercy that comes to us in the very heart of our fear, guilt, and disgrace. Few frame the conundrum in more realistic terms than Romano Guardini. Commenting on First Epistle of St. John: "By this we shall . . . reassure our hearts before him whenever our hearts condemn us; for God is greater than our hearts, and he knows everything," Guardini refuses to sugarcoat offenses against God and likewise won't lessen the pain we feel at having sinned and being unable to retract our sins. It seems like an impossible tension to bear. We have wronged God, and yet,

> . . . His creative love is greater than all this wrong. John [the Apostle] does not say: *Cheer up, it isn't so bad after all*. He does not say: *Don't take life so seriously*. God says: *Give these things their full weight. Then I will come to you. I am God.*
>
> The answer is not: *You have done right. Your intentions were good. Be of good cheer.* No, the answer is: *God is greater than thy heart.*
>
> Thy heart is great. . . . But God is still greater.
>
> There is only one answer which, provided it is really given, answers every question because it puts an end to all questioning: the answer is that He is who He is. May He grant us to know who He is.[10]

As mentioned in chapter eight, St. Paul says in Hebrews that Jesus "who for the joy that was set before him endured the cross, despising the shame, and is seated at the right hand of the throne of God" (12:2). Jesus indeed experienced the shame, humiliation, and pain that sin produces in us. "For our sake he made him to be sin who knew no sin, so that in him we might become the righteousness of God" (2 Cor 5:21). The Lord absorbed all that makes us suffer into himself. Even the sufferings we bring on ourselves due to sin he took upon himself. Even the shame we feel after sin. And this applies to any and every sin committed by everyone.

Jesus comes to us utterly crushed by the evil of this world, and he says: *You think I don't get it? You think this is all an act I'm putting on? You think I don't know how you feel? You think that when you've committed a sin that you are so ashamed of and cannot shake from your memory, that I don't know what that feels like? What do you think was on my heart and mind in Gethsemane? Do you think I was thinking about myself? It was you I was thinking of. It was your guilt and shame that made me sweat blood.*

May he grant us to know who he is. Amen.

ENDNOTES

1. Gregory of Narek, *Speaking with God from the Depths of the Heart: The Armenian Prayer Book of St. Gregory of Narek*, trans. Thomas J. Samuelian, 4th ed. (Vem Press, 2015), Prayer 71.

2. *Catechism*, no. 1505.

3. Hubert van Zeller, *The Choice of God* (Templegate, 1956), p. 161.

4. Benedict XVI, Encyclical on Christian Hope *Spe Salvi* (November 30, 2007), no. 32. https://www.vatican.va.

5. Aquinas, *Summa Theologiae*, 2-2.144.2.

6. John Paul II, General Audience (May 14, 1980), no. 1. https://www.vatican.va.

7. Francis, Homily, "The Grace of Shame" (March 9, 2020). https://www.vatican.va.

8. Carl Jung, *Psychology and Alchemy*, in Bollingen Series XX (Princeton University Press, 1980), p. 36.

9. *The Sayings of the Desert Fathers*, trans. Benedicta Ward (Cistercian, 1975), p. 224.

10. Romano Guardini, *The Living God* (Pantheon, 1957), pp. 57, 59. Emphasis added.

TWELVE

"Do not be anxious"

> Therefore I tell you, do not be anxious about your life, what you shall eat or what you shall drink, nor about your body, what you shall put on. Is not life more than food, and the body more than clothing?
> —Mt 6:25

> Therefore do not be anxious about tomorrow, for tomorrow will be anxious for itself. Let the day's own trouble be sufficient for the day.
> —Mt 6:34

We cannot conclude these reflections without devoting a chapter to anxiety. Of all unwanted thoughts, those that elicit high anxiety or panic are among the most unwanted. They really seem to hijack a person from the inside, making inner peace impossible.

Setting aside the diagnostic categories of the various anxiety disorders, which require special therapeutic interventions, anxiety of a greater or lesser degree remains a staple of daily life for most. Again, it may never reach a clinical level, where daily functioning is impaired, but it is sufficiently present to preoccupy us, make us lose sleep, and compromise our affective energy and cognitive space. It is a significant enough problem that the Lord devoted an entire section of the Sermon on the Mount to its prevention by providing the rationale for releasing needless anxiety: Your Father in heaven sees; your Father in heaven knows; your Father in heaven provides (see Mt 6:25–34). Let him decide when and how your needs should be met.

Prohibition against anxiety is not prohibition against foresight, planning ahead, or preventing problems. Nor is it even close to forbidding wholesome concern for the welfare of others, as when parents "stress" over the moral choices of their children. There is ample material for concern here. The point is to draw a firm boundary between what God enables us to do in the ordinary working of his providence and what is his proper work to do. Call it staying in your own lane. Twelve-Step programs joke pointedly about us trying to do God's job, trying to run the world, making everyone do what they are supposed to do. Self-defeating and unrealistic expectations are often a setup for even more self-defeating coping behavior.

Making reasonable provision for the future, doing our best to encourage others to act morally without making their decisions for them—all with trust in God—can be done without undue anxiety. But it takes much faith and confidence in God. And this is precisely what is asked of us.

It is often observed that anxiety has never been higher or more widespread than in contemporary culture. Social comparison via social media is clearly global. News outlets report nearly all events as urgent, dire, catastrophic, something you should be worried about, numbing us to what we should be genuinely concerned about. All news is "breaking"; every new bit of information is a "must see" or "bombshell." There are clear commercial reasons for this (*keep watching and meanwhile order something from our sponsors*). But it might not be too exaggerated to apply Murray Bowen's description of the family as "living under the same emotional skin" to the world at large—stretching that skin, so to speak, over the entire globe.

Even if the people of Our Lord's time did not live in a global village but lived in actual villages and comparatively small cities, anxiety remained an issue. The objects of excess worry were perhaps not as numerous and certainly not as artificial, but the underlying causes remain the same: As human beings subject to the uncertainties and losses of life, to the changes of seasons, we want security and peace, we want love, and we want to be happy.

We devoted an earlier chapter to original sin and its effects on the soul. One of the most lasting effects is a distrust of God as Father. Will God provide for me? Can I trust him? The serpent had insinuated a decidedly negative answer: that God was keeping the best things from Adam and Eve because he did not want to share his divine privileges with them. We have inherited that lack of confidence. We are tempted to test God, to make him prove himself, before we will trust him.

Jesus repeatedly calls for an extremely high level of trust from his disciples—not only without apology but also with an *in-your-face* quality. He chides the apostles for being terrified as their storm-tossed boat seemed on the verge of sinking, while he had been sleeping on a cushion in the stern.

> And a great storm of wind arose, and the waves beat into the boat, so that the boat was already filling. But he was in the stern, asleep on the cushion; and they woke him and said to him, "Teacher, do you not care if we perish?" And he awoke and rebuked the wind, and said to the sea, "Peace! Be still!" And the wind ceased, and there was a great calm. He said to them, "Why are you afraid? Have you no faith?" (Mk 4:37–40)

Especially remarkable here is the Lord's lack of any reassuring words. Instead we are greeted with a bald-faced challenge to trust, even when circumstances leave practically no other option than panic. The apostles' response to the storm does not seem exaggerated in the least. They thought they were going to die by drowning. But it was precisely in the fury of the tempest and then its sudden calm that Jesus wanted to teach an unforgettable lesson: *Never doubt my loving providence over your life. Never. You will suffer in this world, you will suffer other kinds of storms in life, but remember that I am with you. When you think I should be intervening in one way or another, instead be attentive to how I am actually present and active in the midst of your confusion and fear.*

No promise is made to spare any of them from suffering, but the most solemn promise is made that Jesus will be our Emmanuel, our "God with us," through it all. More than words, the Word became flesh to demonstrate his closeness once and for all.

A cognitive behavioral therapist I know tells his clients burdened by anxiety, panic, and/or phobias that there are no guarantees in life. There is danger. There is harm. Nothing is 100 percent fail-safe. Your boat might sink; your plane may crash; you might suffer a terminal disease. But in keeping with CBT principles, his therapy attempts to bring clients closer to reality: to recognize probabilities versus exceptions, to see the reasonable versus the irrational, to consider likely outcomes versus low-probability outcomes. This is really the only sane way to live in an uncertain world. God does not call us to pretend everything is okay and will always be okay. He calls us to trust in him no matter what happens.

Saints like Anthony of Egypt (ca. 250–350), considered the founder of Western monasticism prior to the organizational structures introduced by St. Benedict of Nursia, acknowledged the fleeting nature of human life and codified not so much an order of life as an attitude of spirit toward it. He instructed his disciples:

> For our life is naturally uncertain, and Providence allots it to us daily. But thus ordering our daily life, we shall neither fall into sin, nor have a lust for anything, nor cherish wrath against any, nor shall we heap up treasure upon earth. But, as though under the daily expectation of death, we shall be without wealth, and shall forgive all things to all men, nor shall we retain at all the desire of women or of any other foul pleasure. But we shall turn from it as past and gone, ever striving and looking forward to the day of Judgment.[1]

The gentle motion of turning away shows the dispositions of mind and heart required for lifelong Christian asceticism. Acknowledging the pull of temptation and the weaknesses to which the flesh is prone, Anthony's light touch recognizes that meeting ferocity with ferocity may cause a stress fracture in the soul. High stress is unsustainable in the long run. Something's got to give.

If this seems counterintuitive, many strategic plans are. In the spiritual life we are not trying to outsmart the adversary, the devil, which we cannot do. We are trying to descend gently into humility, which always conquers the devil. We are adapting our interior struggle to the nature of the players involved. Our memory and imagination do not respond to harsh measures, the way we can chain up a wild beast, and walk safely away. No, each new confrontation requires a consistent, invisible, act of the will saying no to the unhelpful or immoral thought. That incremental movement away from the alluring, fascinating, or disturbing thought is what builds up the soul into a house where God can dwell. It is a brick-by-brick process, humble and hidden, but it is the only way our interior fortress can be built.

We cannot see the final picture, the tapestry, of what God's providence encompasses. And, most importantly, he does not want us to. Hence, "we walk by faith, not by sight" (2 Cor 5:7). We are called to get comfortable not in the dubious securities of the world, but in a pitching boat. Perhaps paradoxically, it is to rest secure in the cradle of Christ's hand: "And I give them eternal life, and they shall never perish, and no one shall snatch them out of my hand. My Father, who has given them to me, is greater than all, and no one is able to snatch them out of the Father's hand" (Jn 10:28–29).

If you scan the New Testament for adverse experiences, you will indeed find them. St. Paul is beaten up, shipwrecked, imprisoned, and if you want to know more, he's prepared to tell you:

> Are they servants of Christ? I am a better one—I am talking like a madman—with far greater labors, far more imprisonments, with countless beatings, and often near death. Five times I have received at the hands of the Jews the forty lashes less one. Three times I have been beaten with rods; once I was stoned. Three times I have been shipwrecked; a night and a day I have been adrift at sea; on frequent journeys, in danger from rivers, danger from robbers, danger from my own people, danger from Gentiles, danger in the city, danger in the wilderness, danger at sea, danger from false brethren; in toil and hardship, through many a sleepless night, in hunger and thirst, often without food, in cold and exposure. And, apart from other things, there is the daily pressure upon me of my anxiety for all the churches. (2 Cor 11:23–28)

Pressures? Anxieties? Persecutions? Is this any way for God to treat an apostle? St. Paul merely recounts and does not judge the providence that has guided his life. He knows too much. Or better, he knows the Lord too well to doubt his providence. He knows how God works to bring about good even when we are nursing wounds sustained in his service. Even more, he trusts him. Paul knows to expect trouble in this world and is prepared to serve the Lord in and through it all. How does he know? Not from the word of others, nor from reading about it. For him, the theoretical stage has passed over to proof: He has ventured out in faith and found God faithful.

Our anxious thoughts might pester us with the idea that it shouldn't be like this. Life should be safe, trouble-free, conflict-free, free from adversity. A world like that does not need redemption. It has no need of an Incarnation, Passion, and Resurrection. In short, it has no need of a Jesus. Accepting the disappointments and insecurities inherent in this valley of tears, we adjust and adapt ourselves to a growth process that adversity occasions. This is the gospel way to view contradiction, trial, and temptation, emboldening St. James to declare:, "Count it all joy, my brethren, when you meet various trials, for you know that the testing of your faith produces steadfastness. And let steadfastness have its full effect, that you may be perfect and complete, lacking in nothing" (Jas 1:2–4).

The point here is to reconcile ourselves to the reality that God places before us and, instead of brooding over injustice, ask more constructively what he wants us to do about it. Anxiety often breeds avoidance. Avoidance is especially a failed strategy for those who are called to die to self, lose self, and carry the cross behind the Lord Jesus. The cross is confrontation. The cross contradicts all of our natural desires for self-preservation and comfort. If we are saved by it, then our salvation is worked out through it, by our willingness to embrace it as best we can each day.

Fr. Gerald Vann, OP, wrote many years ago that we must face dragons in the spiritual life, a common theme in adventure stories and by no means restricted to ancient myth. Rather it is both daily and necessary if we would live as conquerors with Christ. The Book of Revelation alerts us that after having failed to destroy the woman who had given birth to Christ, "Then the dragon was angry with the woman, and went off to make war on the rest of her offspring, on those who keep the commandments of God and bear testimony to Jesus" (12:17). We know who that woman is; we know who her offspring are. We are involved in what you might call the daily working out of an ancient myth as primordial as Eden and as momentous as the trial faced by our first parents, not to mention by the woman and her child. It is the "daily death" of which St. Paul speaks, but always in view of new life born from the old (see 1 Cor 15:31).

> If we set out along the road that leads to God, and to the loving union of our will with the will of God, we cannot get far without meeting a dragon.
>
> In the myths of the world, this theme of the hero who sets out on a dark journey and must meet and slay a dragon is recurrent. You find it again in the works of the poets. And all these statements of the theme are statements of what man knows in his deepest self to be the truth about humanity: there is something within us that has to be fought and slain before we can find life. We must, as our Lord told Nicodemus, be born again before we can come to the kingdom of God.[2]

Each anxiety we experience reveals a dragon of sorts, a fearsome specter we wish would just crawl away and die. But *we* must kill it. It doesn't die of natural causes; it feeds on them. The Lord's promise that his disciples will "tread upon serpents and scorpions" (Lk 10:19) is much more than a literal guarantee to imperviousness against deadly creatures. These creatures represent moral, physical, emotional, and spiritual trials that conspire to deter the disciple from bravery in the service of the gospel. The point is to cultivate approach over avoidance, confidence over hesitancy, courage over fear.

A total change of outlook is called for. The metanoia referenced earlier is that global transformation of thought, affection, and action. Why? Because Jesus has changed the game, flipped the script, by giving us the firmest causes for hope, faith, and love. And he is the cause. His love, life, passion, death, and resurrection invert the fallen world into something redeemed and continually redeemable.

St. John Paul II once called the bluff of those who say that high Christian ideals are only ideals and thus unattainable for most people. In addressing the particularly delicate area of procreation and contraception, he laid bare the terms:

> It would be a very serious error to conclude . . . that the Church's teaching is essentially only an "ideal" which must then be adapted, proportioned, graduated to the so-called concrete possibilities of man, according to a "balancing of the goods in question." But what are the "concrete possibilities of man"? And of which man are we speaking? Of man *dominated* by lust or of man *redeemed* by Christ? This is what is at stake: the *reality* of Christ's redemption. *Christ has redeemed us!* This means

> that he has given us the possibility of realizing the *entire* truth of our being; he has set our freedom free from the *domination* of concupiscence. And if redeemed man still sins, this is not due to an imperfection of Christ's redemptive act, but to man's will not to avail himself of the grace which flows from that act. God's command is of course proportioned to man's capabilities; but to the capabilities of the man to whom the Holy Spirit has been given; of the man who, though he has fallen into sin, can always obtain pardon and enjoy the presence of the Holy Spirit.[3]

The fact that life in this world is unideal is news to no one. But it might serve to recall that it is here, and nowhere else, where "the full truth of our being" is actualized. What we call our "self" is constantly in need of testing, of both failure and success, of the experience of both our weakness and strength, so that the truly Christian self can emerge. We strive for the ideal in the midst of ruins, chaos, temptation, and adversity, and grace makes it all possible. We discover our true selves and our true purpose in the struggle.

Jesus came to save an unideal and hostile world. He brought life to the dead, hope to the despairing, strength to the weak. Every good we could ask for is found most perfectly in him. Our task, our adventure, is to build a universal culture where gospel ideals are at least acknowledged as such, even if not consistently observed. And this begins in our own head.

Creating a Christian culture in your mind is the first step to contributing to the transformation of your environment. Your thinking, evaluating, and judging all need to be thoroughly imbued with the spirit of Christ and the grace of the gospel.

The process is one of deep reception of the Word of God. Reading, meditating, and implementing, after the manner of the rich soil that receives the seed of God's Word and produces abundant fruit. Some practical advice for processing the Word of God in a way that can also help mitigate anxiety is journaling or diary-keeping. This strategy employs both personal and dialogical dimensions, and is a form of prayer, as is evidenced by the writings of many saints.

When in a state of anxiety, it is wise to take pen and journal in hand and tell the Lord what you are feeling and why you think you are feeling that way. As you write, you analyze your thoughts in a more objective way, ordering them by externalizing them on paper. Instead of being a victim of an oppressive thought loop, you are breaking the tight circle of rumination by letting it out and, thus, you reduce some of the inner pressure occasioned by the anxious thoughts.

But journaling need not be an emergency measure only. Writing out a Scripture verse, pondering its applications to your life, and then sketching some practical conclusions treats Scripture as a living text, capable of giving practical direction to your life. Simultaneously, you are training your mind and imagination to meditate lovingly over God's Word as something intended for you.

As you work through the personal transformation prayer inspires, you will begin to see how God alone fulfills you, how all other attempts at explaining the "meaning of life" fail to varying degrees.

Secular psychology typically demurs from answering the more metaphysical questions regarding man's final end, life after death; in the absence of empirical evidence, most remain silent and stick to functionality as the human ideal. Beyond functioning, perhaps occasional experiences of "transcendence" might be as far as we can go: quasi-ecstatic self-forgetfulness in rewarding activities, the experience of nature and art—perhaps these are the best and highest experiences human life can hope to attain.

But the metaphysical questions are exactly the ones we want answered. I know what it's like to be transported by Bach, to be rapt by artful cinema and great works of art and literature. This is not the question, nor is it the answer. The ultimate root of human anxiety is not only the lack of assurance of meaning in this life, but of ultimate meaning beyond this one. Fear and trembling should indeed come upon us if the only answer we get from the experts is that daily functioning is more or less the best we can hope for.

Don't get me wrong: Daily functioning is no small thing. It is not a trivial goal. But neither does it exhaust the purpose of man's existence and destiny. Animals and insects function quite well, but listen to what Jesus has to say about the issue: "Fear not; you are of more value than many sparrows" (Lk 12:7). If our dignity surpasses theirs, then surely our ultimate destiny possesses a greater value as well. Far lesser things, such as "the grass which is alive in the field today and tomorrow is thrown into the oven" (Lk 12:28) are given as signs that God so values our dignity as to clothe us, not only in this life but more mysteriously and permanently in the next:

> For while we are still in this tent, we sigh with anxiety; not that we would be unclothed, but that we would be further clothed, so that what is mortal may be swallowed up by life. He who has prepared us for this very thing is God, who has given us the Spirit as a guarantee. (2 Cor 5:4–5)

I will only trust the word of someone who has died and come back to tell me that there are dwelling places that he has prepared. I will only trust someone who actually died for me and then returned to tell me that his death has freed me from the fear and power of death. I will only trust someone whose promises are written in his own blood. I will only trust someone who tells me that heaven is best compared to a wedding banquet, where eternal union with Love itself is the end goal. Any other finality produces not only anxiety but full existential dread in my soul.

Anyone who has ever loved another knows the strength of preoccupation with the beloved. Fascination, joy, comfort—all continually revolve in the mind. To the extent that the love is honorable and pure, to that extent is trust engendered, and to that extent is anxiety banished. There is no longer room for it. David was a man in love, a man who knew himself to be loved and forgiven by God, and his testimony rings true for all beset by adversity yet who enjoy an overriding confidence in God:

> The Lord is my light and my salvation;
>   whom shall I fear?
> The Lord is the stronghold of my life;
>   of whom shall I be afraid?

When evildoers assail me,
    uttering slanders against me,
my adversaries and foes,
    they shall stumble and fall.
Though a host encamp against me,
    my heart shall not fear;
though war arise against me,
    yet I will be confident.
One thing have I asked of the Lord,
    that will I seek after;
that I may dwell in the house of the Lord
    all the days of my life,
to behold the beauty of the Lord,
    and to inquire in his temple.
For he will hide me in his shelter
    in the day of trouble;
he will conceal me under the cover of his tent,
    he will set me high upon a rock.
And now my head shall be lifted up
    above my enemies round about me;
and I will offer in his tent
    sacrifices with shouts of joy;
I will sing and make melody to the Lord.
Hear, O Lord, when I cry aloud,
    be gracious to me and answer me!
Thou hast said, "Seek ye my face."
    My heart says to thee,
"Thy face, Lord, do I seek."
    Hide not thy face from me.

Turn not thy servant away in anger,
thou who hast been my help.
Cast me not off, forsake me not,
O God of my salvation!
For my father and my mother have forsaken me,
but the LORD will take me up.
Teach me thy way, O LORD;
and lead me on a level path
because of my enemies.
Give me not up to the will of my adversaries;
for false witnesses have risen against me,
and they breathe out violence.
I believe that I shall see the goodness of the LORD
in the land of the living!
Wait for the LORD;
be strong, and let your heart take courage;
yea, wait for the LORD! (Ps 27)

Following directly from Psalm 27, the wisdom of our Desert Fathers returns for a final word. Abbot Abraham, in the twenty-fourth and final of Cassian's conferences, presents a sophisticated analogy of love as the architectural fulcrum for our spiritual edifice, the house of the soul:

> A monk's whole attention should thus be fixed on one point, and the rise and circle of all his thoughts be vigorously restricted to it; viz., to the recollection of God, as when a man, who is anxious to raise on high a vault of a round arch, must constantly draw a line round from its exact centre, and in accordance with the sure

standard it gives discover by the laws of building all the evenness and roundness required. But if anyone tries to finish it without ascertaining its center, though with the utmost confidence in his art and ability, it is impossible for him to keep the circumference even, without any error, or to find out simply by looking at it how much he has taken off by his mistake from the beauty of real roundness, unless he always has recourse to that test of truth and by its decision corrects the inner and outer edge of his work, and so finishes the large and lofty pile to the exact point.

So also our mind, unless by working round the love of the Lord alone as an immovably fixed centre, through all the circumstances of our works and contrivances, it either fits or rejects the character of all our thoughts by the excellent compasses, if I may so say, of love, will never by excellent skill build up the structure of that spiritual edifice of which Paul is the architect, nor possess that beautiful house, which the blessed David desired in his heart to show to the Lord and said: *"I have loved the beauty of Your house and the place of the dwelling of Your glory."*[4]

ENDNOTES

1. Athanasius of Alexandria, *Life of St. Antony*, trans. H. Ellershaw, in *Nicene and Post-Nicene Fathers*, Second Series, vol. 4, ed. Philip Schaff and Henry Wace (Buffalo, NY: Christian Literature, 1892), no. 19, accessed at http://www.newadvent.org/fathers/2811.htm.

2. Gerald Vann, *Taming the Restless Heart* (Sophia Institute Press, 1999), p. 25.

3. John Paul II, quoting an address to those taking part in a course on "responsible parenthood," March 1, 1984, in Encyclical *Veritatis Splendor* (August 6, 1993), no. 103. https://www.vatican.va.

4. John Cassian, "The Conference of Abbot Abraham on Mortification," in *Nicene and Post-Nicene Fathers*, Second Series, vol. 11, p. 531.